American History
Historical Outline Map Book
With Lesson Ideas

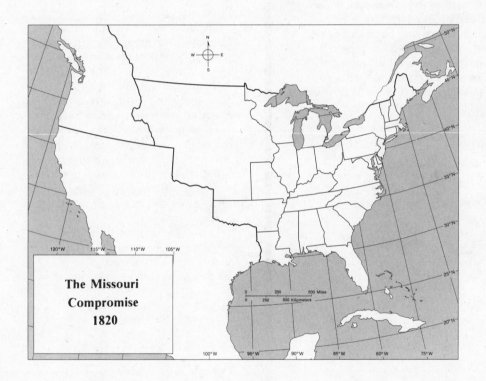

The Missouri
Compromise
1820

Prentice
Hall

Upper Saddle River, New Jersey
Glenview, Illinois
Needham, Massachusetts

American History
Historical Outline Map Book
With Lesson Ideas

2002 Printing

ISBN 0-13-062912-X

3 4 5 6 7 8 9 10   06 05 04 03 02

Prentice
Hall

TO THE TEACHER

This book contains 92 outline maps. The first 70 of these are historical outline maps of important developments in American history, including European explorations, the American Revolution, United States expansion, and United States post–World War II policy.

Maps 71 to 81 are outline maps of current world regions. These maps are especially useful when teaching about United States foreign policy. Maps 82 to 92 are outline maps of the United States today, including regional maps that can be used to teach state and local history.

These maps are designed for use in your American history class. By completing the maps and analyzing the results, students will gain both valuable geography skills and an understanding of American history and its relationship to geography.

Lesson ideas are included in the book for each map; however, because the maps are outline maps, the possibilities for use in your class are limitless.

CONTENTS

Lesson Ideas

1 Hunters Reach America

1. Have students use their text or a reference map to locate and label the following:

North America	South America
Asia	Pacific Ocean
Atlantic Ocean	Bering Sea
Bering Strait	Rocky Mountains
Appalachian Mountains	

2. Ask students to use different colors or different patterns to shade the areas where glaciers existed and where a land bridge was exposed during the last ice age.

3. Have them draw the routes taken by ancient peoples who crossed the land bridge from Asia to North and South America.

4. Have them create a key in the blank box.

5. Ask: (a) In what directions did the ancient people travel when they crossed the land bridge? (b) What happened to the land bridge across which these people traveled? (c) Through which mountain range did ancient people travel in western North America? In eastern North America?

6. Critical Thinking (a) Why might these people have left Asia? (b) What factors would have led to their survival in North and South America?

2 Physical Regions of the United States

1. Have students use their text or a reference map to locate and label the following:

Cascades	Appalachian Mountains
Mississippi River	Central Plains
Hawaii	Sierra Nevada
Pacific Ocean	Lake Ontario
Lake Erie	Great Plains
Gulf Plain	Alaska
Lake Superior	Lake Huron
Atlantic Plain	Rio Grande
Lake Michigan	Rocky Mountains
Atlantic Ocean	Gulf of Mexico

2. Ask students to use different colors or different patterns to shade the nine physical regions of the United States:

Pacific Coast	Interior Plains
Rocky Mountains	Coastal Plains
Appalachian Mountains	Ozark Highlands
Canadian Shield	Hawaii
Intermountain	

3. Have them create a key in the blank box.

4. Ask: (a) Which river runs north–south? (b) Which physical region is the largest?

5. Critical Thinking (a) Based on your map, which regions of the United States are probably sparsely populated? (b) Which parts are probably densely populated? Explain. Use a population distribution map to check your answers.

3 Climates of the United States

1. Have students use their text or a reference map to locate each climate region described below. Then have them label each region with the name and the letter of the description.

A. In this climate region near the North and South Poles, the winters are very cold and the summers are very short.

B. At one time, buffalo herds grazing on the plains were common to this climate region with its very hot summers and very cold winters.

C. People of the Central Plains and northeastern United States experience the hot summers and cold winters of this region.

D. This climate region is typical of mountainous areas with high elevations.

E. This climate region's dry heat is perfect for cactus, but other plants require irrigation.

F. The coast of California is the only place in the United States where this climate region's mild, wet winters and sunny, dry summers are found.

G. Humid summers and mild winters make this climate region a good place to grow cotton, tobacco, and peanuts.

H. This hot, rainy, steamy climate region is known to people in Hawaii and in the southern tip of Florida.

I. Lands south of the North Pole, such as Alaska, experience the short summers and cold winters of this climate region.

J. This climate region's mild, rainy weather is found on the northwestern coast of the United States.

2. Ask students to shade each climate region with a different color or different pattern.

3. Have them create a key in the blank box.

4. Ask: (a) In which climate region do you live? (b) Which state has the greatest number of climate regions?

5. Critical Thinking In what ways would the economy of a region be affected by its climate? You may wish to check a reference map that shows economic activity across the United States.

4 Native American Cultures

1. Have students use their text or a reference map to identify and label the Native American culture regions outlined on the map.
2. Ask students to use different colors or different patterns to shade each region.
3. Have them create a key in the blank box.
4. Tell students to identify at least two Native American nations in each culture region. Then have them write the names of the nations in the appropriate region on the map.
5. **Critical Thinking** In what ways do Native American cultures reflect environmental influences?

5 Great Empires of the Americas

1. Have students use their text or a reference map to locate and label the following:

Mississippi River	Caribbean Sea
North America	Rio Grande
Pacific Ocean	Andes Mountains
South America	Rocky Mountains
Amazon River	Atlantic Ocean

2. Ask students to use different colors or different patterns to shade the empires of the Aztec, Maya, and Inca.
3. Have students locate and label the cities of Tenochtitlan, Tikal, and Cuzco.
4. Have them create a key in the blank box.
5. Ask students to study a map of present-day Latin America. Then ask: (a) What countries exist where the Aztec, Maya, and Inca empires once did? (b) What city is located near the spot where Tenochtitlan once was?
6. **Critical Thinking** (a) Why do you think the Inca empire extended north and south and not east? (b) How might the geographic nature of the Inca empire have created problems for the government?

6 To India By Sea

1. Have students use their text or a reference map to locate and label the following:

Portugal	Spain
Mediterranean Sea	Asia
Indian Ocean	India
Africa	Cape of Good Hope
Gold Coast	Europe
Cape Bojador	Atlantic Ocean
Niger River	

2. Ask students to locate and label the cities of Lisbon, Sagres, and Timbuktu.
3. Tell students to use different colors or different patterns to shade the area of the kingdoms of Songhai and Kanem-Bornu. Then have them use matching rules to show the borders of Ghana and Mali.
4. Have them use different colors or patterns to draw the routes Bartholomeu Dias and Vasco da Gama took to explore the coast of Africa.

5. Have students create a key in the blank box.
6. Ask students which of the following statements are supported by the map. Then have them correct the incorrect statements.

A. Bartholomeu Dias sailed all the way around the coast of Africa to India.
B. The Gold Coast lies north of the equator and the Cape of Good Hope lies south of it.
C. On the way to Asia, da Gama sailed around the Cape of Good Hope.
D. Timbuktu is located on the Niger River.
E. Spain was the first European country to reach India by an all-water route.
F. The African kingdoms of Mali and Songhai controlled a portion of the Atlantic coast.
G. Portuguese explorers sailed an all-water route to Asia through the Mediterranean Sea.
H. The city of Sagre is located at about 8°N/38°W.

7. **Critical Thinking** Agree or disagree with the following statement: "Portugal was bound to be the first European nation to discover an all-water route to Asia." Support your position with information from the map and your text.

7 Columbus Reaches America

1. Have students use their text or a reference map to locate and label the following:

West Indies	North America
South America	Europe
Portugal	Caribbean Sea
Spain	Canary Islands
Cape Verde Islands	Africa
Atlantic Ocean	

2. Ask students to use different colors or different patterns to draw lines showing the four voyages that Columbus took to America.
3. Have them create a key in the blank box.
4. Ask: (a) In which direction did Columbus sail to get from Europe to the New World? (b) On which voyage did Columbus stop at the Cape Verde Islands? (c) At approximately what latitude and longitude are the Canary Islands?
5. **Critical Thinking** Why did Columbus think he had reached the East Indies?

8 Voyages of Discovery

1. Have students use their text or a reference map to locate and label the following:

North America	Africa
Line of Demarcation	Europe
Pacific Ocean	India
Australia	Cape of Good Hope
South America	Asia
Cape Horn	Philippine Islands
Atlantic Ocean	Indian Ocean

2. Ask students to decide which European nation each explorer listed below sailed for. Have them chose a different color or line pattern for each country; then use it to show the routes taken by the following:

Cabral (1500)
Magellan (1519–1522)
Dias (1487)
Columbus (1492, 1493, 1498, and 1502)

Balboa (1513)
Drake (1579–1580)
da Gama (1497–1498)

3. Have them create a key in the blank box.
4. Ask: (a) Which explorers circumnavigated the globe? (b) Which explorers sailed for Spain? Portugal? England? (c) Which explorers sailed around Cape Horn? Around the Cape of Good Hope? (d) Through which continents does the Line of Demarcation pass?
5. Critical Thinking Is it correct to say that the European explorers shown on your map "discovered" North and South America or the East Indies? Explain.

9 Spanish Explorers in North America

1. Have students use their text or a reference map to locate and label the following:

Colorado River
Pacific Ocean
Gulf of Mexico
Cuba
Florida
Caribbean Sea

Arkansas River
Rio Grande
Mississippi River
Hispaniola
Atlantic Ocean
Mexico City

2. Ask students to use different colors or patterns to draw the routes of the following Spanish explorers:

Ponce de León (1513)
Narváez/De Vaca (1528–1536)
Coronado (1540–1547)

Cortés (1519–1521)
De Soto (1539–1542)

3. Have them create a key in the blank box.
4. Ask students which of the statements below are supported by the map. Then have them correct the incorrect statements.

A. Narváez's and De Vaca's expedition journeyed through Mexico City.
B. Hispaniola is closer to Florida than it is to the island of Cuba.
C. De Soto explored the Florida peninsula.
D. Coronado explored Hispaniola and Cuba.
E. Ponce de León sailed down the Mississippi.
F. De Soto's expedition crossed the Mississippi River.
G. Narváez sailed the northern coast of the Gulf of Mexico.
H. Cortés sailed through the Caribbean Sea and the Gulf of Mexico.

5. Critical Thinking How do you think Spain was affected by the accomplishments of the Spanish conquistadors and explorers?

10 Search for a Northwest Passage

1. Have students use their text or a reference map to locate and label the following:

North America
Hudson Bay
Iceland
England
France
Atlantic Ocean
Hudson River

Africa
Greenland
Newfoundland
Netherlands
Spain
St. Lawrence River

2. Ask students to use different colors or different patterns to shade England, France, and the Netherlands. Then have them use matching colors or patterns to draw the routes of the following explorers:

Cabot (1497)
Cartier (1534)
Hudson (1609)

Verrazano (1524)
Frobisher (1576–1577)
Hudson (1610)

3. Have them create a key in the blank box.
4. Ask: (a) Which explorer sailed along the Atlantic coast of North America? (b) Which explorer sailed the St. Lawrence River? (c) Which explorer made voyages for two European nations? (d) Which explorer sailed farthest south? (e) Did the explorers on your map sail north or south of the equator? East or west of the prime meridian?
5. Critical Thinking (a) What did European countries hope to find when they sent explorers to North America? (b) Suggest reasons why countries in eastern Europe did not send expeditions to North America.

11 Spain and Portugal in the Americas

1. Have students use their text or a reference map to locate and label the following:

Atlantic Ocean
Caribbean Sea
Brazil
Viceroyalty of Peru

Pacific Ocean
West Indies
Viceroyalty of New Spain
Line of Demarcation

2. Ask students to use one color or pattern to shade the area controlled by Spain and another color or pattern to shade the area controlled by Portugal. Then have them locate and label the following cities:

St. Augustine
Lima

Bahia
Mexico City

Valparaiso

3. Have them create a key in the blank box.
4. Ask: (a) At approximately what latitude and longitude is Mexico City? Bahia? (b) At approximately what longitude does the Line of Demarcation fall? (c) In whose territory does the city of St. Augustine fall?
5. Critical Thinking Review a reference map showing the geography of South America. Why do you think the claims of both Spain and Portugal were limited mostly to coastal areas?

12 The French Explore North America

1. Have students use their text or a reference map to locate and label the following:

Atlantic Ocean
Lake Superior
Lake Michigan
Lake Ontario
St. Lawrence River
Mississippi River
Ohio River
Louisiana
English Colonies

Gulf of Mexico
Lake Huron
Lake Erie
Lake Champlain
Nova Scotia
Florida
Missouri River
New France

2. Ask students to locate and label the following cities:

Quebec
Montreal
New Orleans

Port Royal
Fort Detroit

3. Have students use different colors or different patterns to draw the exploration routes taken by Champlain (1608), Marquette and Joliet (1673), and La Salle (1682).
4. Ask: (a) Which explorers sailed down the Mississippi River? (b) Which explorer sailed the St. Lawrence River? (c) Into which body of water does the Mississippi River flow? (d) At approximately what latitude and longitude is the mouth of the St. Lawrence River?
5. **Critical Thinking** Why do you think the cities of Quebec, Montreal, Fort Detroit, and New Orleans have survived to present times?

13 New Netherland and New Sweden

1. Have students use their text or a reference map to locate and label the following:

Atlantic Ocean
Hudson River
New Amsterdam
Fort Christina
Delaware Bay

Delaware River
Fort Orange
Long Island
Breuckelen

2. Ask students to use one color or pattern to shade the area of New Netherland and another color or pattern to shade the area of New Sweden.
3. Have them create a key in the blank box.
4. Ask: (a) Into which body of water does the Hudson River flow? The Delaware River? (b) In what direction would one have to travel to get from New Amsterdam to Fort Christina?
5. **Critical Thinking** What geographic factors make the locations of New Netherland and New Sweden suitable for settlement?

14 The First English Settlements

1. Have students use their text or a reference map to locate and label the following:

Appalachian Mountains
Cape Cod
Chesapeake Bay
Hudson River
James River

Virginia
Atlantic Ocean
Delaware River
Potomac River
Roanoke River

2. Ask students to locate and mark with a symbol the colonies of Roanoke, Jamestown, and Plymouth.
3. Have students locate and label the areas where the following Indians lived:

Wampanoag
Susquehanna
Tuscarora
Delaware

Narraganset
Powhatan
Iroquois

4. Have them create a key in the blank box.
5. Ask: (a) Based on your map, with which Indian group would Plymouth colony be most likely to come into contact? (b) Which Indian groups lived near the Appalachian Mountains? (c) Into which present-day states do Roanoke, Jamestown, and Plymouth fall?
6. **Critical Thinking** Imagine that you obtained a charter to colonize land in America. (a) What geographic and climatic qualities would you want in your location? (b) What supplies would you bring from home? (c) What types of skills would you want the other colonists to possess? (d) How do you think Indian groups in your settlement area will react to your presence? (e) How do you plan to approach these Indian groups?

15 The Thirteen Colonies

1. Have students use their text or a reference map to locate and label the following:

New York
Massachusetts
Connecticut
Pennsylvania
New Jersey
Virginia
South Carolina
Maine
Lake Superior
Lake Erie
Lake Huron
Ohio River
Delaware River
Hudson River
Appalachian Mountains

New Hampshire
Georgia
Rhode Island
Delaware
Maryland
North Carolina
Florida
Louisiana
Lake Michigan
Lake Ontario
Mississippi River
James River
Potomac River
St. Lawrence River

2. Have students locate and label the following cities:

Savannah	Charleston
Jamestown	Baltimore
Philadelphia	New York
Hartford	Newport
Providence	Boston

3. Ask students to use different colors or different patterns to shade the New England Colonies, the Middle Colonies, the Southern Colonies, the area claimed by Spain, the area claimed by France, the area claimed by both France and the colonies, and the area claimed by New York and New Hampshire.

4. Have them create a key in the blank box.

5. Ask: (a) What natural barrier forms the western border of the Southern Colonies? (b) What state now exists in the area claimed by New York and New Hampshire? (c) What river forms the natural border between Maryland and Virginia?

6. Critical Thinking Why was access to waterways an important factor in the development of colonial cities and towns? Based on your map, give examples of cities located near rivers.

16   The New England Colonies

1. Have students use their text or a reference map to locate the colonies described below. Ask them to label each place with its name and the letter of the description.

A. John Winthrop was the first governor of this colony.
B. The Connecticut River is this New England colony's western border, and Massachusetts is its southern border.
C. Thomas Hooker, founder of this colony, believed in government by the consent of the governed.
D. Roger Williams established this colony on the principle of toleration of religion.

2. Have students use their text or a reference map to locate and label the following:

Maine	Lake Champlain
Hudson River	Atlantic Ocean
Kennebec River	Connecticut River
Narragansett Bay	Cape Cod
Massachusetts Bay	New Haven
Hartford	Providence
Newport	Boston
Plymouth	Springfield
Falmouth	St. Lawrence River

3. Ask students to create a symbol for each of the following New England industries: Grain, Cattle, Lumber, Fish, Whales, Furs, Ships, Iron, and Rum. Have them use their text or a reference map to find out where these industries thrived during colonial times.

Then have students use the symbols to show where these industries were located.

4. Have them create a key in the blank box.

5. Ask: (a) What river runs through Connecticut and Massachusetts? (b) In which direction would you travel to get from New Haven to Boston by land? By ship? (c) In which colonies was the fur trade established?

6. Critical Thinking Why do you think the ship-building industry was important to New England?

17   The Middle Colonies

1. Have students use their text or a reference map to locate the colony described in each of the statements below. Ask them to label each place with its name and the letter of the description.

A. This proprietary colony, situated between the Hudson and Delaware rivers, was founded in 1664.
B. This colony was originally settled by Swedes, captured by the Dutch, and then controlled by the colony of Pennsylvania.
C. In 1664, the Dutch surrendered this colony to the English without firing a shot.
D. William Penn founded this colony so that Quakers and other religious sects could practice their religion freely.

2. Have students use their text or a reference map to locate and label the following:

Lake Ontario	Lake Erie
Perth Amboy	New York City
Dover	Wilmington
Appalachian Mountains	Albany
Schenectady	Lancaster
Philadelphia	Long Island
Lake Champlain	Hudson River
Susquehanna River	Delaware River
St. Lawrence River	

3. Ask students to create a symbol for each of the following Middle Colony industries: Grain, Cattle, Lumber, Fish, Rum, and Iron. Have them use their text or a reference map to find out where these industries thrived during colonial times. Then have students use their symbols to show where these industries were located.

4. Have them create a key in the blank box.

5. Ask: (a) Which industries exist in the colony of New York? (b) In which colonies could an iron miner find employment? (c) Into which body of water does the Susquehanna River run?

6. Critical Thinking How did the Middle Colonies differ geographically and economically from the New England and Southern Colonies?

18 The Southern Colonies

1. Have students use their text or a reference map to locate the colony described in each of the statements below. Ask them to label each place with its name and the letter of the description.

A. This colony's southern neighbor is Georgia.
B. Lord Baltimore was given this colony by King Charles I as a proprietary colony.
C. This colony is the northern portion of a land grant that was named after King Charles II.
D. General James Oglethorpe encouraged former debtors to immigrate to this colony.
E. This colony's House of Burgesses was the first representative assembly in the New World.

2. Have students use their text or a reference map to locate and label the following:

Appalachian Mountains	Baltimore
St. Mary's	Williamsburg
Jamestown	Cape Hatteras
Wilmington	Charleston
Savannah	Altamaha River
St. Augustine	Atlantic Ocean
Roanoke River	Savannah River
James River	Potomac River
Norfolk	Chesapeake Bay

3. Ask students to create a symbol for each of the following Southern Colony industries: Rice, Grain, Indigo, Cattle, Tobacco, Lumber, Fish, Rum, and Iron. Have them use their text or a reference map to find out where these industries thrived during colonial times. Then have students use their symbols to show where these industries were located.
4. Have them create a key in the blank box.
5. Ask: (a) In which colony is the city of Charleston located? (b) Through which colony does the James River run? (c) In which colonies is tobacco a major industry? (d) Where is rice generally planted?
6. **Critical Thinking** How did differences in the geography of the tidewater region and the backcountry region affect the way of life in the two regions?

19 Major Trade Routes

1. Have students use their text or a reference map to locate and label the following:

North America	Europe
Africa	West Indies
Atlantic Ocean	England
Boston	New York
Philadelphia	Charleston

2. Ask students to use three different colors or patterns to show trade routes (a) between England and the American colonies; (b) between England and the West Indies; and (c) among the American colonies, the West Indies, and West Africa. Tell students to indicate on their maps what products were traded on each route.
3. Have them create a key in the blank box.
4. Ask students which of the following statements are supported by the map. Have them correct the incorrect statements.

A. Slaves were bought and sold on the triangular trade routes.
B. New York City is located along a latitude of 42 °S.
C. The colonies provided England with manufactured goods.
D. Slaves were shipped from West Africa to the West Indies.
E. Rice and tobacco were shipped to England from the Southern Colonies.
F. The city of Charleston is located along a longitude of 80 °W.
G. The colonies traded only with England.

5. **Critical Thinking** (a) Based on your map, explain why trade among the colonies, the West Indies, and West Africa was called the triangular trade. (b) Why did England try to control colonial trade?

20 North America in 1753

1. Copy the following sentences on the chalkboard or duplicate them and distribute copies. Have students fill in the blanks with the name of the place described. Then have them use the outline map and their text or a reference map to locate and label each area with its name and the letter of the description.

A. Russia claimed the northern area of _____ , but the larger part of this northwest region of North America remained unexplored.
B. The French named _____ after King Louis XIV.
C. On the west coast of _____ _____ was the Pacific Ocean and on the east coast was the Gulf of Mexico.
D. Ponce de Leon had explored _____ in search of the Fountain of Youth.
E. The islands in the Caribbean Sea were called the _____ .
F. The St. Lawrence River was part of _____ _____ .
G. _____ , a British territory, was located between the latitudes of 15 °N and 18 °N and was surrounded by Spanish territory.
H. The _____ _____ were located along the Atlantic coastline.
I. The _____ River flows from a latitude of about 47 °N and empties into the Gulf of Mexico.

2. Have students locate and label the following cities: Quebec, Boston, Charleston, New Orleans, El Paso, and Mexico City.
3. Ask students to use different colors or different patterns to shade in the territories claimed by Britain, France, Spain, and Russia.

4. Have them create a key in the blank box.

5. Ask: (a) Which European nation claimed Alaska? (b) Which European nations claimed lands on the coast of the Gulf of Mexico? (c) Which European nations had direct access to the Pacific Ocean? (d) What is the latitude and longitude of El Paso? Of New Orleans? (e) Which nation controlled Quebec?

6. **Critical Thinking** (a) Which nation(s) would the British be most likely to come into conflict with in the New World? Explain. (b) Why do you think control of the Mississippi River was important during the mid-1700s?

21 The French and Indian War

1. Have students use their text or a reference map to locate and label the following:

New France	New Hampshire
Massachusetts	New York
Connecticut	Rhode Island
Pennsylvania	New Jersey
Delaware	Maryland
Virginia	Allegheny River
Lake Erie	Lake Ontario
St. Lawrence River	Hudson River
Lake Champlain	Ohio River

2. Ask students to locate and label the cities of Albany, Boston, Port Royal, Halifax, Montreal, and Quebec.

3. Tell students to locate and label the following French forts: Ft. Duquesne, Ft. Frontenac, Ft. Niagara, Ft. Crown Point, Ft. Louisbourg, Ft. Owsego, and Ft. Ticonderoga. Then have them locate and label the following British forts: Ft. Necessity, Ft. William Henry, and Ft. Cumberland. Have students use different colors or symbols to distinguish between French and British forts.

4. Ask students to draw lines showing British advances on the French during the French and Indian War.

5. Have them create a key in the blank box.

6. Ask: (a) From what directions did the British approach Montreal? (b) Across which lake did British forces sail to attack Fort Frontenac? (c) From what city did the British launch their attack on Ft. Oswego?

7. **Critical Thinking** Based on your map, explain why the control of waterways was important in the French and Indian War.

22 North America in 1763

1. Have students use their text or a reference map to locate and label the following:

Canada	Alaska
Louisiana	New Spain
13 Colonies	Honduras
Mississippi River	West Indies
Gulf of Mexico	

2. Ask students to locate and label the following cities: Santa Fe, New Orleans, Charleston, Detroit, Quebec, and New York.

3. Tell students to use different colors or different patterns to shade in the areas claimed by Britain, France, and Spain, and the area claimed by Russia, Spain, and Britain.

4. Have them create a key in the blank box.

5. Ask: (a) Which nation had the smallest land claim in North America in 1763? (b) Which nation controlled the Great Lakes? (c) What is the latitude and longitude of Quebec? Of Santa Fe? Of Charleston? (d) Which nation claimed Detroit?

6. **Critical Thinking** Have students compare this map with one of North America in 1753. Ask: (a) In 1763, which European nation would Britain be most likely to come into conflict with in the New World? Explain. (b) Describe how the situation in North America had changed between 1753 and 1763.

23 Lexington and Concord

1. Have students use their text or a reference map to locate and label the following:

Boston	Lexington
Charlestown	Cambridge
Charles River	North Bridge
Old North Church	Menotomy
Concord River	Concord

2. Ask students to use one color or pattern to draw the routes taken by Revere, Dawes, and Prescott to Concord. Have them use another color or pattern to show the British advance on Concord and retreat from Concord. Tell students to locate and label each battle site with a symbol.

3. Have them create a key in the blank box.

4. Ask: (a) Which river runs under the North Bridge? (b) Where did Revere and Dawes meet? (c) In which direction did the British travel from Boston to Concord?

5. **Critical Thinking** Based on your map, why was the location of the Old North Church a good choice for a signal point?

24 The Revolutionary War: An Overview

1. Have students use their text or a reference map to locate the place described in each of the phrases below. Ask them to label each place with its name and the letter of the description.

A. fort located on Lake Champlain

B. place where "the shot heard round the world" was fired

C. New Jersey city with a latitude and longitude of 40 °N/75 °W

D. city placed under seige by British troops

E. city where the Continental Congress met
F. colony directly affected by the Intolerable Acts
G. city found at a latitude and longitude of 37°N/76°W
H. colony whose northern and western borders were Lake Ontario and Lake Erie
I. colony whose assembly was dismissed by the royal governor in 1774
J. colony whose representatives to the Continental Congress included Joseph Galloway and John Dickenson

2. Ask: (a) What was the latitude of New York's northern border? (b) In what direction would one travel to get from Boston to Philadelphia by land? (c) What is the latitude and longitude of Philadelphia? Of Concord?
3. Critical Thinking (a) How might the geography of the American colonies have affected the war strategy of the Americans? Of the British? (b) For which side would the size of the colonies have been an advantage?

25 The Revolutionary War in the Northeast

1. Have students use their text or a reference map to locate and label the following:

New York	New Jersey
Pennsylvania	Delaware
Maryland	Lake Champlain
Lake Ontario	Hudson River
Delaware River	Chesapeake Bay
New York City	Valley Forge
Morristown	Albany
Montreal	Quebec
Ft. Oswego	Ft. Stanwix
St. Lawrence River	

2. Ask students to locate and label the following battle sites using one color or symbol if the battle was an American victory and another color or symbol if it was a British victory.

Bennington	Saratoga
Oriskany	Ft. Ticonderoga
Long Island	Princeton
Trenton	Philadelphia
Brandywine	

3. Tell students to draw the routes taken by American and British troops from 1776 to 1777. Have them use one color or pattern to draw the routes of American generals Washington, Arnold, and Gates and another color or pattern to draw the routes of British generals Cornwallis, Howe, Burgoyne, and St. Leger. Ask students to label each route with the correct general's name.
4. Have them create a key in the blank box.
5. Ask students which of the statements below are supported by the map. Then have them correct the incorrect statements.

A. St. Leger traveled down the St. Lawrence River on the way from Montreal to Ft. Oswego.
B. Howe sailed up the Chesapeake Bay on his way to Brandywine.
C. Cornwallis fought Washington at Philadelphia.
D. The Battle of Long Island was won by the British.
E. Ft. Ticonderoga was taken from the British by General Arnold.
F. The battles of Trenton and Philadelphia took place in Pennsylvania.
G. Washington and his troops took Trenton before moving on to battle at Princeton.
H. Burgoyne went from Quebec to Ft. Ticonderoga and then to Saratoga.

6. Critical Thinking (a) How did both the British and Americans take advantage of waterways in the colonies? (b) Who do you think made the best use of the waterways? Explain.

26 The Revolutionary War in the West

1. Have students use their text or a reference map to locate and label the following:

Fort Detroit	Fort Miami
Fort Pitt	Ohio River
Wabash River	Lake Michigan
Mississippi River	Lake Erie
Appalachian Mountains	

2. Ask students to locate and label the following battle sites: Cahokia, Kaskaskia, and Vincennes. Have them use a different color or symbol to indicate whether the battle was a British or an American victory.
3. Have students use different colors or different patterned lines to show the routes of Clark's troops and Hamilton's troops.
4. Have them create a key in the blank box.
5. Ask: (a) At which forts were Clark and Hamilton based? (b) Which river did Clark follow to Kaskaskia? (c) Which river did Hamilton follow to Vincennes? (d) Where do you think the roughest part of Clark's march to Kaskaskia was? Explain. (e) Where did Clark and Hamilton do battle?
6. Critical Thinking Explain the effect American victories in the West might have had after the Revolutionary War.

27 The Revolutionary War in the South

1. Copy the following sentences on the chalkboard or duplicate them and distribute copies. Have students fill in the blanks with the place or places described. Then have them use their text or a reference map to locate and label each area with its name and the letter of the description.

A. The cities of Richmond and Yorktown are located on the _____ River.
B. Cornwallis won battles at _____ and _____ in South Carolina.
C. The _____ Bay lies on the western coast of Maryland.
D. The last battle of the Revolutionary War was fought in the town of _____ .
E. Cornwallis marched from _____ in North Carolina to _____ in Virginia, where he was victorious.
F. Washington's and Rochambeau's armies met in the city of _____ and from there marched to Virginia.
G. The border between Maryland and Virginia is formed by the _____ River.
H. The _____ Mountains stretch from Georgia to Maine.

2. Ask students to draw the following routes on their maps, using one color or pattern to show the routes of the British troops and another color or pattern to show the routes of the American troops.

A. Cornwallis's advances in South Carolina and North Carolina
B. Cornwallis's advance on Richmond
C. De Grasse's naval advance on the Chesapeake Bay
D. Washington and Rochambeau's attack on Yorktown
E. Lafayette and Wayne's move on Richmond and Yorktown

3. Have them create a key in the blank box.
4. Ask: (a) In which direction did Washington and Rochambeau's troops travel from New York? (b) Which rivers did Cornwallis's troops cross between the battles of Charleston and Richmond?
5. **Critical Thinking** Agree or disagree with the following statement: "Control of the Atlantic coastline was a vital factor in the American victory at Yorktown." Defend your position with information from your map and text.

28 North America in 1783

1. Have students use their text or a reference map to locate and label the following:

Alaska	Canada
United States	Louisiana
New Spain	West Indies
Mississippi River	Rio Grande
Caribbean Sea	Gulf of Mexico
Florida	

2. Ask students to use different colors or different patterns to shade the United States, British territory, French territory, Spanish territory, territory claimed by both the United States and Spain, territory claimed by both the United States and Britain, and territory claimed by Russia, Spain, and Britain. Then have them indicate the area of the original 13 states.

3. Have them create a key in the blank box.
4. Ask students which of the following statements are supported by the map. Then have them correct the incorrect statements.

A. Spain claimed Louisiana.
B. The French had no claims in Canada.
C. Both the United States and France claimed an area northwest of Florida.
D. France and Spain shared Hispaniola.
E. Spain claimed land along the west coast from Alaska to South America.
F. Russia and France claimed Alaska.

5. **Critical Thinking** (a) Based on your map, approximately how much larger was the United States than the 13 colonies? (b) What benefits did the additional land probably bring? What challenges did the additional land probably pose?

29 Western Land Claims

1. Have students use their text or a reference map to locate and label the following:

Maine	Massachusetts
New Hampshire	Vermont
Rhode Island	Connecticut
New Jersey	New York
Pennsylvania	Maryland
Delaware	Virginia
North Carolina	South Carolina
Georgia	Western Reserve
Northwest Territory	
Florida	

2. Ask students to locate and label Virginia's land claims, North Carolina's land claims, and Georgia's land claims; lands claimed by the United States, Georgia, and Spain; and lands ceded to the United States by South Carolina.
3. Have them use different colors or different patterns to shade the area of the United States, the claimed territories, and the Northwest Territory.
4. Have them create a key in the blank box.
5. Ask: (a) Which states had not ceded their western land claims to the United States by 1787? (b) Which European nation claimed the same land claimed by the United States? (c) Which state claimed the Western Reserve?
6. **Critical Thinking** Based on your map, what geographic features of the Northwest Territory made it valuable to the United States?

30 Exploring the Louisiana Purchase

1. Have students use their text or a reference map to locate the places described in the statements below. Then ask them to label each place with its name and the letter of the description.

A. Before 1803, this nation's eastern and western boundaries were defined by the Atlantic Ocean and the Mississippi River.
B. Jefferson sent representatives to France to buy this city.
C. This mountain range is North America's continental divide.
D. This territory was claimed by Britain, Russia, Spain, and the United States.
E. Napoleon sold the United States this territory in order to finance his European wars.
F. The Rio Grande and the Great Salt Lake were two bodies of water in this region.
G. Lewis and Clark began their expedition from this city.
H. St. Augustine, the oldest European settlement in the United States, was in this territory.
I. Lewis and Clark followed this river when they explored the territory the United States had recently purchased.

2. Ask students to use different colors or different patterns to show the route of Lewis and Clark's expedition (1804–1806) and the routes of Pike's two expeditions (1805–1806 and 1806–1807).
3. Have them create a key in the blank box.
4. Ask: (a) Whose expedition went into Spanish territory? (b) Which city lay at the mouth of the Mississippi River? (c) At approximately what latitude and longitude is St. Louis? (d) Whose expedition traveled to a longitude of approximately 124°W?
5. **Critical Thinking** Jefferson stated in his first inaugural address that the United States was "kindly separated by nature and a wide ocean from the exterminating havoc of one quarter of the globe." (a) After studying this map and reading about the Louisiana Purchase, do you agree or disagree with Jefferson? Explain. (b) Do you think the Louisiana Purchase further isolated the United States from Europe or brought the two worlds closer? Explain.

31 Land Acquired From Native Americans to 1810

1. Have students use their text or a reference map to determine where the following Native American peoples lived in 1810. Then have students locate and label these places on their outline maps.

Shawnee	Iroquois
Delaware	Chickasaw
Seminole	Natchez
Mohegan	Cherokee
Miami	Creek
Kansas	Illinois

2. Ask them to label the Mississippi River, the Ohio River, and the Red River.
3. Tell students that the map outlines the land acquired from Native Americans during three periods of time: (a) before 1750; (b) between 1750 and 1783; and (c) between 1784 and 1810. Have students use different col-

ors or different patterns to shade the land lost by Native Americans during each of these three periods of time.
4. Have them create a key in the blank box.
5. Ask students which of the statements below are supported by the map. Then have them correct the incorrect statements.

A. The Iroquois lived west of the Mississippi River.
B. Between 1750 and 1783, Seminole Indians lost land along the Florida coast.
C. White settlers began acquiring land west of the Mississippi River before 1750.
D. The Natchez lived near the Red River.
E. The Shawnee lived south of the Miami.
F. As early as 1750, white settlers claimed territory on which the Delaware Indians lived.
G. The Mohegan live farther from the Ohio River than the Chickasaw did.

6. **Critical Thinking** (a) Based on your map, describe the pattern of white settlement between 1750 and 1810. (b) How did access to waterways affect white settlement? (c) Which Indian nations were probably threatened with losing land to white settlements after 1810? Explain.

32 The War of 1812

1. Have students use their text or a reference map to locate the places described in the statements below. Then ask them to label each place with its name and the letter of the description.

A. Due to the skill and courage of Captain Perry, a battle on this lake was an American victory in 1813.
B. This region was the British stronghold in North America in 1812.
C. In 1814, the British burned this capital city.
D. Andrew Jackson fought the Creek Indians in this territory.
E. The British attacked New Orleans by sailing through this body of water.
F. Captain Macdonough won control of this lake from the British.
G. After three days of bombardment, the British could not win control of Fort McHenry, which is located in this city.
H. In the last battle of the war, the British tried to take New Orleans, which is located at the mouth of this river.

2. Ask students to locate and label the individual states of the United States. Have them also draw a dashed line to indicate the British naval blockade.
3. Have students locate and label the following battle sites using one color or symbol if the battle was an American victory and another color or symbol if it was a British victory.

Horseshoe Bend	Ft. McHenry
Lake Erie	New Orleans
Plattsburgh	The Thames

4. Have them create a key in the blank box.

5. Ask: (a) Why did the British want to control New Orleans? (b) Which bodies of water did the British navy blockade? (c) In which part(s) of the United States did most of the battles of the War of 1812 take place?

6. Critical Thinking (a) Explain how your map demonstrates a relationship between the War of 1812 and westward expansion. (b) How do you suppose a victory for the British at New Orleans would have affected the conditions of the Treaty of Ghent? Explain.

33   Transportation to the West

1. Have students use their text or a reference map to locate and label the states and territories outlined on their maps. Then have them locate and label the following:

Lake Erie	Hudson River
Ohio River	Mississippi River
Wabash River	Appalachian Mountains
Cumberland Gap	

2. Ask students to locate and label the following cities:

Portland	Philadelphia
Baltimore	Richmond
St. Augustine	St. Louis
Louisville	Nashville
Albany	Buffalo
Toledo	Evansville
Cincinnati	Pittsburgh
New Orleans	

3. Have students use one color or pattern to show the routes of the following canals:

Erie (Albany to Buffalo)
Wabash and Erie (Toledo to Evansville)
Miami and Erie (Toledo to Cincinnati)
Pennsylvania (Philadelphia to Pittsburgh)

Have them use another color or pattern to show the routes of the following roads:

National Road (Baltimore to St. Louis)
Coastal Post Road (Portland to St. Augustine)
Wilderness Road (Richmond to Louisville)
Nashville Road (Richmond to Nashville)

4. Have them create a key in the blank box.

5. Ask: (a) In what direction was the National Road built? (b) What water systems does the Erie Canal link? (c) What roads, canals, and rivers would be used to send a shipment from Portland to New Orleans? From Toledo to Louisville? From Buffalo to St. Louis?

6. Critical Thinking (a) What kinds of geographical ''obstacles'' did road and canal builders have to confront? (b) How might the construction of roads and canals affect the natural geographic features of the lands on which they were built?

34   The United States in 1824

1. Copy the following sentences on the chalkboard or duplicate them and distribute copies. Have students fill in the blanks with the name of the area described. Then have them use their text or a reference map to locate and label each area with its name and the letter of the description. Ask students to use different colors or different patterns to shade each area.

A. The large territory north of the United States called _____ was controlled by the British.

B. In 1824, the _____ Territory was occupied by Britain and the United States.

C. In the Adams-Onís Treaty of 1819, Spain ceded _____ to the United States.

D. After 1819, the largest Spanish territory in North America was _____ .

2. Ask students to locate and label each state and each territory shown on the outline map. Have them use a color or pattern to shade the states admitted to the Union after 1790.

3. Have them create a key in the blank box.

4. Ask: (a) Which mountain range divided the first 13 states from the newer states? (b) How many new states had been admitted to the Union by 1824? (c) Which nations controlled the Great Lakes?

5. Critical Thinking (a) How might future settlement of the Oregon Territory by the United States be affected by the Rocky Mountains? (b) Based on your map, which nation seems to have an advantage in making a claim to the Oregon Territory, Britain or the United States? Explain.

35   New Nations in Latin America

1. Have students use their text or a reference map to locate and label the following:

Mexico	Haiti
Santo Domingo	Honduras
Guatemala	El Salvador
Nicaragua	Costa Rica
Panama	Colombia
Venezuela	Ecuador
Peru	Brazil
Bolivia	Paraguay
Chile	Argentina
Uruguay	Atlantic Ocean
Pacific Ocean	Gulf of Mexico

2. Have them use their reference source to find out when each of these Latin American nations achieved independence.

3. Ask students to shade the areas that were still claimed by European nations in 1825.

4. Have them create a key in the blank box.

5. Ask students which of the statements below are supported by the map. Have them correct the incorrect statements.

A. Nicaragua had access to the Pacific Ocean and the Caribbean Sea.
B. Brazil won its independence after Chile did.
C. The west coast of Chile lies along a longitude of approximately 71°E.
D. Cuba gained its independence in 1821.
E. Peru is south of Colombia.
F. Haiti was the first Latin American nation to gain independence.
G. Venezuela's northern border lies along a latitude of approximately 10°N.
H. The equator goes through Brazil and Argentina.

6. Critical Thinking How might geography have contributed to the formation of many small nations in Central and South America as opposed to the formation of a few large nations in North America?

36 Election of 1828

1. Have students use their text or a reference map to locate and label the states shown on the outline map.
2. Tell students that they will be preparing a map that shows the results of the election of 1828. Using their text or another source, have students use one color or pattern to shade the states Andrew Jackson won and another color or pattern to shade the states John Quincy Adams won.
3. Have them create a key in the blank box.
4. Ask students which of the statements below are supported by the map. Have them correct the incorrect statements.

A. Jackson won all of the states along the eastern seaboard.
B. Indiana's electors voted for Jackson.
C. New York's electors voted for Adams.
D. Adams won most of Maine's electors.
E. Jackson was supported by the Southern states.
F. Jackson won the election of 1828 by a landslide.
G. Adams won the state of Alabama.
H. Jackson and Adams split the electors of Missouri.

5. Critical Thinking Based on your map, decide whether the election of 1828 showed evidence of sectionalism. Explain why or why not.

37 Indian Removal, 1830–1842

1. Tell students that they will be preparing a map showing the effect of the Removal Act of 1830. Have students use their text or a reference map to locate and label each state outlined on the map, the Mississippi River, and the Gulf of Mexico.
2. Ask students to use different colors or different patterns to label and/or shade the areas where the following Indian nations lived before 1830:

Seminole	Cherokee
Creek	Chickasaw
Choctoaw	Shawnee
Miami	Potawatomi

3. Then have students shade the area given to the Indians and label it "Indian Territory."
4. Using matching colors or patterns, have students show the routes each Indian nation traveled to the Indian Territory.
5. Have them create a key in the blank box.
6. Ask: (a) In which states did the Cherokee live before 1830? (b) Which Indian nations lived in the Great Lakes area before 1830? (c) Which Indian nation had to cross the Gulf of Mexico after 1830? (d) Which Indian nations lived in Mississippi before 1830? (e) In which general direction did all the Indians have to move after passage of the Removal Act?
7. Critical Thinking Why did Congress choose the specific site that they did for the Indian Territory?

38 Oregon Country

1. Have students use their text or a reference map to locate each area described in the phrases below. Then have them label each area with its name and the letter of its description.

A. country from which the Oregon Trail originated
B. territory claimed by Russia
C. country that won independence from Spain in 1821
D. territory located north of the latitude 54°40′N and controlled by Britain
E. territory split between Britain and the United States at the latitude of 49°N

2. Ask students to locate and label the following places on their maps:

Astoria	Fort Vancouver
Columbia River	Snake River
Vancouver Island	Fort Victoria
South Pass	

3. Have students draw a line showing the boundaries established at the 49th parallel between the United States and Britain in 1818 and in 1846. Then tell students to draw the route of the Oregon Trail.
4. Ask students to shade the area of Oregon Country that had been settled by 1840.
5. Have them create a key in the blank box.
6. Ask: (a) In what mountain range was the South Pass located? (b) At what parallel was the boundary between Oregon Country and Mexico? (c) On which river was Astoria built? (d) What is the approximate latitude and longitude of Fort Victoria?
7. Critical Thinking (a) Why do you think the settled portion of Oregon Country was so small in 1840? (b) Why did American settlers outnumber British settlers there?

39 Independence for Texas

1. Have students use their text or a reference map to locate and label the following:

Republic of Texas   United States
Mexico   Gulf of Mexico
Red River   Rio Grande
Nueces River

2. Ask students to locate and label the following battles. Have them use one color or symbol to indicate a Texan victory and another color or symbol to indicate a Mexican victory.

Goliad   San Antonio
the Alamo   Gonzales
San Jacinto

3. Have students shade the area claimed by both Texas and Mexico. Then ask them to use different colors or different patterns to show the routes of the Texan army and the routes of the Mexican army.

4. Have them create a key in the blank box.

5. Ask students to decide whether the statements below are supported by the map. Have them correct the incorrect statements.

A. Santa Anna's forces crossed the Rio Grande.

B. Gonzales was a victory for the Texans.

C. The battle at San Jacinto took place near the Atlantic Ocean.

D. The Alamo was a victory for the Mexican forces.

E. After their victory at Gonzales, Houston's army retreated to San Jacinto.

F. The Mexican army followed the Texans from Gonzales to Goliad.

G. Mexican forces traveled south from Mexico to reach Texas.

6. Critical Thinking (a) Based on your map, would you say the Texans were fighting an offensive or a defensive war? Explain. (b) What do you think are the advantages and disadvantages of offensive wars? Of defensive wars?

40 Trails to the West

1. Have students identify the place or places described in the statements below. Then ask them to locate and label each place on their outline maps.

A. This republic won its independence from Mexico in 1836.

B. Entrance to this region could be gained through the South Pass and by following the Snake and Columbia rivers.

C. This country won its independence from Spain in 1821.

D. This mountain range posed a challenge to settlers who went west in the 1800s.

E. In 1818, the United States and Britain agreed to draw a border at the 49th parallel, between the United States and this region.

2. Ask students to locate and label the following forts and cities:

Nauvoo   St. Louis
Independence   Ft. Dodge
Ft. Laramie   Salt Lake City
Ft. Walla Walla Portland
Sutter's Fort   Los Angeles
San Diego   El Paso
San Francisco

3. Then have them locate and label the following rivers and mountain passes: Rio Grande, Platte River, Snake River, Columbia River, Donner Pass, and South Pass.

4. Ask students to use different colors or patterns to show the following trails:

   Mormon Trail (Nauvoo to Salt Lake City)
   Oregon Trail (Independence to Portland)
   California Trail (Independence to Sutter's Fort)
   Santa Fe Trail (Independence to Santa Fe)
   Old Spanish Trail (Santa Fe to Los Angeles)
   Gila River Trail (Santa Fe to San Diego)
   Butterfield Overland Mail Trail (St. Louis to San Francisco)

5. Have them create a key in the blank box.

6. Ask: (a) In which general direction did the trails go? (b) Through which mountain pass did people travel to get to Sutter's Fort? (c) Which trails began at Santa Fe? (d) Which trail passed through Los Angeles? (e) Where did the Mormon Trail end? (f) Which trail did people take to get to Portland?

7. Critical Thinking Point out to students that most groups of pioneers set up a government with an elected captain before they started west. Have students imagine that they are captains of a group of westbound pioneers. Tell them to answer the following questions: (a) What is your group's destination? (b) On which trail will you travel? (c) What kinds of skills do you hope the people in your group have? (d) What kinds of supplies will you bring? (e) How will you prepare for meetings with Indian groups? (f) What do you think the most difficult part of your journey will be? Why?

41 War With Mexico, 1846–1848

1. Have students use their text or a reference map to locate and label the following:

Mexico   United States
California   San Francisco
Monterey   Los Angeles
San Diego   Pacific Ocean
Gulf of Mexico   Texas
Louisiana   Arkansas
Rio Grande   Ft. Leavenworth

2. Ask students to shade the area claimed by both the United States and Mexico. Then have them label the following battle sites, using different colors or symbols to indicate whether the battle was an American victory or a Mexican victory: Mexico City, Buena Vista, Monterrey, and Veracruz.

3. Tell students to use one color or pattern to show the routes of American forces led by Fremont, Stockton, Sloat, Kearny, Taylor, and Scott. Have them use another color or pattern to show the routes of Mexican forces led by Santa Anna, Ampudia, and Arista.

4. Have them create a key in the blank box.

5. Ask: (a) At what latitude and longitude is Ft. Leavenworth? Los Angeles? Mexico City? (b) Which army won the battle at Monterrey? (c) Approximately how many miles did Kearny's army travel from Ft. Leavenworth to San Diego?

6. Critical Thinking (a) Why did United States strategy in the war with Mexico work successfully? (b) What parts of the strategy were based on geography?

42 Growth of the United States to 1853

1. Point out to students that their maps have been divided into eight regions representing stages in United States expansion. Have students use their text or a reference map to identify and locate each region described in the statements below. Then have them label each region with its name, the year it became part of the United States, and the letter of the description.

A. Congress annexed this territory in 1845 by a joint resolution.

B. In 1846, Britain agreed to United States control of this territory south of the 49th parallel.

C. This territory was acquired in 1848 through the Treaty of Guadalupe-Hidalgo.

D. In 1853, the United States bought this territory from Mexico for $10 million.

E. The United States purchased this large territory from France in 1803.

F. One result of the Convention of 1818 was British cession of this territory to the United States.

G. Spain ceded this territory to the United States in 1819.

H. This territory represents United States expansion to 1783.

2. Have students use their outline maps to answer the following questions. Ask: (a) Which states were carved from the Mexican Cession? (b) When did the area of your state become part of the United States? (c) Which nations originally claimed that territory? (d) Can you find evidence of that nation's influence today? Give examples.

3. Critical Thinking (a) How does your map illustrate the idea of "manifest destiny"? (b) What do you think Mexico and Britain thought about manifest destiny? Explain.

43 The Northern States

1. Have students use their text or a reference map to locate and label the following states:

Maine	Vermont
New Hampshire	Rhode Island
Massachusetts	Connecticut
New York	Pennsylvania
New Jersey	Delaware
Ohio	Michigan
Indiana	Wisconsin
Illinois	Iowa
Minnesota	

2. Tell students to create symbols to represent the following industries: textiles, iron and steel, mining, lumber, cattle, and grain. Have them use their text or a reference source to find out where these industries flourished in the North during the mid-1800s. Then ask students to use the symbols to label their maps.

3. Have them create a key in the blank box.

4. Ask students which of the following statements are supported by the map. Have them correct the incorrect statements.

A. Most of the states around the Great Lakes had lumber industries.

B. The mining industry probably had an important impact on Michigan's economy.

C. Cattle herds were raised mainly in the New England states.

D. New Jersey and Delaware had iron and steel industries.

E. Textiles were produced mainly in states on the Atlantic Coast.

5. Critical Thinking (a) How did local geography affect the development of the industries shown on your map? (b) How do you think the types of industries that flourished in the North influenced the lifestyle there?

44 The Southern States

1. Have students use their text or a reference map to locate and label the following states:

Maryland	Virginia
Kentucky	North Carolina
South Carolina	Tennessee
Georgia	Alabama
Mississippi	Missouri
Arkansas	Louisiana
Texas	Florida

2. Tell students to create symbols to represent the following industries: textiles, iron and steel, mining, lumber, cattle, tobacco, rice and sugar cane, cotton, and grain. Have them use their text or a reference source to find out where these industries flourished in the South during the mid-1800s. Then ask students to use the symbols to label their maps.

3. Have them create a key in the blank box.

4. Ask: (a) What industries contributed to Kentucky's economy? (b) In which states was cotton a major industry? (c) Which industries thrived in Texas? (d) Where were rice and sugar cane grown?

5. Critical Thinking (a) How does your map support the following statement: "Cotton was king in the South"? (b) Compare this map to one showing products of the North. How did the economies of the North and South differ?

45 The Missouri Compromise, 1820

1. Have students use their text or a reference map to locate and label the states and territories outlined on their maps.
2. Ask students to use one color or pattern to shade free states in 1820 and another color or pattern to shade slave states in 1820.
3. Tell students to use a solid line to show the Missouri Compromise line. Have them use the colors or patterns from 2. above to shade the territories where slavery was prohibited and where it was allowed according to the Missouri Compromise.
4. Have them create a key in the blank box.
5. Ask students which of the following statements are supported by the map. Have them correct the incorrect statements.

A. Pennsylvania was a free state in 1820.
B. According to the Missouri Compromise, slavery would be prohibited in the Michigan Territory and permitted in the Arkansas Territory.
C. In 1818, the slave states held most of the seats in the Senate.
D. The Missouri Compromise allowed slavery in the Michigan Territory.
E. Florida Territory was slave territory because it was south of the latitude 36°30′.
F. Most of the Louisiana Purchase was south of the Missouri Compromise line.

6. Critical Thinking (a) How did settlement of the West increase tension between the North and the South? (b) What information on the map demonstrates this growing tension? (c) How would the formation of states in the Michigan, Arkansas, and Florida territories probably affect the balance that the Missouri Compromise tried to maintain?

46 The Compromise of 1850

1. Have students use their text or a reference map to locate the area or areas described in each phrase below. Then have them label each area with its name and the letter of the description.

A. two territories that could choose to become slave states through popular sovereignty according to the Compromise of 1850
B. first territory from the Mexican Cession to ask for admission to the nation
C. territory set aside for Indians
D. territory divided at the 49th parallel in an agreement with Britain

2. Ask students to locate and label the remainder of the states and territories outlined on their maps. Then have students use a solid line to show the Missouri Compromise line.
3. Have students use different colors or patterns to shade each of the following: (1) free states and territories in 1850; (2) slave states and territories in 1850; (3) territories open to slavery by popular sovereignty under the Compromise of 1850.
4. Have them create a key in the blank box.
5. Ask: (a) How many free states existed in 1850? How many slave states? (b) Which territories were affected by the Compromise of 1850? How were they affected? (c) How did the number of free states and slave states affect representation in Congress?
6. Critical Thinking Explain why the Missouri Compromise line did not provide a solution to the problem of California's statehood.

47 The Kansas-Nebraska Act, 1854

1. Have students label and locate the states and territories outlined on their maps. Then have them use a line to show the Missouri Compromise line.
2. Ask students to use different colors or patterns to shade (1) free states and territories in 1854; (2) slave states and territories in 1854; (3) territory open to slavery by popular sovereignty according to the Compromise of 1850; (4) territory open to slavery by popular sovereignty according to the Kansas-Nebraska Act of 1854.
3. Have them create a key in the blank box.
4. Ask students which of the following statements are supported by the map. Have them correct the incorrect statements.

A. Missouri was a free state because it was north of the Missouri Compromise line.
B. The New England states were free states.
C. States carved from the Nebraska Territory were to decide on slavery through popular sovereignty.
D. Slavery was allowed in the Utah Territory according to the Compromise of 1850.
E. The Kansas-Nebraska Act repealed the Compromise of 1850.

5. Critical Thinking Support or refute the following statement: "Compromises over slavery were destined to fail because Southerners were fighting for more than slavery; they were trying to preserve a way of life." Defend your position with facts.

48 Election of 1860

1. Have students use their text or a reference map to locate and label the states and territories outlined on their maps.
2. Ask students to use different colors or patterns to shade the states won by the following presidential candidates in the election of 1860: Lincoln, Douglas, Breckinridge, and Bell.
3. Have them create a key in the blank box.

4. Ask students which of the following statements are supported by the map. Have them correct the incorrect statements.

A. Lincoln's main support came from the northern states.
B. Douglas won the second largest number of states.
C. Bell won some of the border states.
D. Georgia and Alabama supported Breckinridge.
E. Electors in the state of California voted for Lincoln.

5. Critical Thinking Explain how this map demonstrates the effect of sectionalism on the election of 1860.

49   Choosing Sides

1. Have students use their text or a reference map and label the states and territories outlined on their maps.
2. Ask students to use different colors or patterns to shade the following areas: (1) free states; (2) slave states loyal to the Union; (3) states that seceded from the Union before April 14, 1861; (4) states that seceded from the Union after April 14, 1861.
3. Have them create a key in the blank box.
4. Ask: (a) Before April 14, 1861, which states were part of the Confederate States of America? (b) Which states were known as border states?
5. Critical Thinking Why did both the Union and the Confederacy try to gain the loyalty of the border states?

50   Major Battles of the Civil War

1. Have students locate and label the states outlined on their maps, the Mississippi, Tennessee, and Cumberland rivers, and the Appalachian Mountains. Ask them to use different colors or patterns to shade Union states and Confederate states.
2. Copy the following sentences on the chalkboard or duplicate them and distribute copies. Have students fill in the blanks with the names of the battle sites described below. Then have them use their text or a reference map to locate and label each site with its name and the letter of the description.

A. The Battle of _____ _____ in July 1861 was the first battle to take place in Virginia.
B. The Confederate army's attack on Fort _____ signaled the start of the Civil War.
C. General Grant captured Fort _____ on the Tennessee River and Fort _____ on the Cumberland River in February 1862.
D. Generals Johnston and Beauregard tried to defeat Grant near _____ , a county meeting house in Tennessee.
E. _____ , the capital of the Confederacy, fell to Union troops in April 1865.
F. On September 17, 1862, McClellan and Lee clashed at _____ , marking one of the bloodiest days in the war.

G. At the Battle of _____ , General Meade forced Confederate troops to retreat from Pennsylvania.
H. After a six-week seige, the city of _____ surrendered to Grant's army.
I. General Sherman destroyed most of the city of _____ , Georgia, as part of the strategy of ''total war.''
J. General Lee surrendered to General Grant at _____ _____ on April 9, 1865.

3. Ask students to use solid lines to show how Scott's anaconda strategy divided the Confederacy into three major theaters of war. Then have them use a dotted line to show the North's naval blockade.
4. Have them create a key in the blank box.
5. Ask: (a) Which battles took place in the eastern theater of the war? (b) Which battles were fought in Tennessee? (c) What is the approximate latitude and longitude of Shiloh? Of Gettysburg?
6. Critical Thinking (a) How did Scott's anaconda strategy use geography? (b) Explain how the naval blockade affected the South.

51   The Civil War in the East

1. Have students use their text or a reference map to locate and label the following:

Richmond	Washington, D.C.
Maryland	Pennsylvania
West Virginia	Virginia
James River	York River
Potomac River	Chesapeake Bay

2. Ask students to locate and label the following battle sites using one color or symbol if it was a Union victory and another color or symbol if it was a Confederate victory.

Seven Days' Battle	Harpers Ferry
Antietam	Fredericksburg
Chancellorsville	Gettysburg
Bull Run	

3. Have students use matching colors or patterns to show the following routes of the Union and Confederate armies:

Lee's advance to Antietam
McClellan's attack on Lee at Antietam
Lee's attack on Gettysburg
Meade's defense of Gettysburg

4. Have them create a key in the blank box.
5. Ask: (a) Which battles were fought on Union territory? On Confederate territory? (b) Which battles were fought on the peninsula between the James and York rivers? (c) Which battle took place farthest north?
6. Critical Thinking What effect did geography have on the outcome of the Battle of Gettysburg?

52 Union Advances

1. Have students use their text or a reference map to locate and label the states outlined on their maps. Then have them locate and label the following:

Richmond	Nashville
Savannah	Ft. Sumter
Appalachian Mountains	Mississippi River
Tennessee River	Cumberland River

2. Ask students to locate and label the following battle sites using one color or symbol if it was a Union victory and another color or symbol if it was a Confederate victory.

Ft. Donelson	Ft. Henry
Shiloh	Memphis
Jackson	Vicksburg
New Orleans	Port Hudson
Chattanooga	Atlanta

3. Have students use matching colors or patterns to show the following routes of the Union and Confederate armies.

Grant's series of victories along the
   Mississippi River in the West
Beauregard's defense of Shiloh
Sherman's "march to the sea"
Bragg's advance from Atlanta to Chattanooga

4. Have them create a key in the blank box.
5. Ask students which of the following statements are supported by the map. Have them correct the incorrect statements.

A. Grant's army captured Shiloh.
B. Bragg's army successfully defended Atlanta.
C. Sherman marched southeast from the Appalachian Mountains to the Atlantic Ocean.
D. Grant conducted a series of campaigns in the West.
E. The Battle of Vicksburg was fought in Alabama.

6. **Critical Thinking** Explain the significance of the Mississippi River during the Civil War. Why was control of this river important?

53 Reconstruction

1. Have students use their text or a reference map to locate and label the states outlined on their maps.
2. Ask them to use a solid line to show the boundary of the Confederate States of America.
3. Tell students that they will be illustrating some of the effects of Radical Reconstruction. Have students use their information source to find out when each former Confederate state was readmitted to the Union. Then have them find out when each state established a conservative government to replace the Reconstruction government.
4. Ask students to label each southern state with the date it was readmitted to the Union and the date its conservative government was established. Tell them to create a way to distinguish between the two dates so that it is clear which date is which.
5. Have them create a key in the blank box.
6. Ask: (a) When was Texas readmitted to the Union? (b) When was a conservative government established in North Carolina? (c) Which state was the last to be readmitted to the Union? (d) Which states were the first to establish conservative governments? (e) In which state did Radical Reconstruction last the longest?
7. **Critical Thinking** How do you think reconstruction efforts in the South affected national elections after the Civil War?

54 Election of 1876

1. Have students use their text or a reference map to locate and label the states outlined on their maps.
2. Ask students to use their information source to find out the results of the election of 1876. Then have them use different colors or patterns to shade the states won by Rutherford B. Hayes, the states won by Samuel Tilden, and the states whose results were disputed.
3. Have them create a key in the blank box.
4. Ask students which of the following statements are supported by the map. Have them correct the incorrect statements.

A. Tilden won the electors in most of the states west of the Mississippi River.
B. Hayes claimed victory in Pennsylvania.
C. Texas electors supported Hayes.
D. The election results in Louisiana, Florida, and South Carolina were disputed.
E. The Republicans were strong in the South, while the Democrats drew support from the North.

5. **Critical Thinking** Based on your map, support or refute the following statement: "The end of the Civil War brought an end to sectionalism." Explain.

55 Indian Lands After 1850

1. Have students use their text or a reference map to locate each place described below. Then have them label it with its name and the letter of the description.

A. fort in Wyoming where a treaty between the United States government and Native Americans was signed in 1851
B. place where Colonel John Chivington destroyed a Cheyenne village and killed 450 Cheyennes
C. location of a battle in which Custer was defeated by the Sioux and Cheyenne
D. site of a tragic battle in which about 200 Sioux and 30 United States soldiers died after a surrender by the Sioux

2. Tell students that they will be using their outline maps to show the land lost by Indians from 1850 to 1890. Have students use different colors or patterns to

shade land lost by Indians (1) before 1850; (2) from 1850 to 1870; (3) from 1870 to 1890. Then have them shade the locations of Indian reservations in 1890.

3. Have them create a key in the blank box.

4. Ask: (a) In which states did battles occur? (b) In which states did the Indians lose land from 1870 to 1890?

5. Critical Thinking (a) Based on your map, write a paragraph describing the pattern in which Indians lost land from 1850 to 1890. (b) Why do you think the treaties between the United States government and the Indian nations did not usually work?

56   Opening the West

1. Have students use their text or a reference map to locate and label the following:

New Orleans	San Antonio
Promontory Point	Los Angeles
San Francisco	Portland
Chicago	Cheyenne
Abilene	Kansas City

2. Ask students to create a symbol and use it to label the following mining centers: Comstock Lode, Boulder, Colorado Springs, Denver, Deadwood, Helena, and Silver City.

3. Tell students to use one color or pattern to show the routes of the following railroads: Central Pacific, Union Pacific, Southern Pacific, and Kansas Pacific.

4. Have them use a second color or pattern to show the routes of the following cattle trails: Goodnight-Loving Trail, Western Trail, Chisholm Trail, and Shawnee Trail.

5. Have students create a key in the blank box.

6. Ask students which of the following statements are supported by the map. Have them correct the incorrect statements.

A. Cattle ranchers on the Goodnight-Loving Trail could ship their cattle on the Union Pacific line.

B. Promontory Point was the meeting place of the Central Pacific and the Kansas Pacific railroad lines.

C. The Southern Pacific railroad went from New Orleans to San Antonio and then to Denver.

D. Most of the railroads traveled east-west while most of the cattle trails went north-south.

E. The Rocky Mountains prevented the construction of a transcontinental railroad.

F. The Central Pacific went through California, Nevada, and Utah.

G. Ranchers who used the Shawnee Trail or the Chisholm Trail could ship cattle on the Kansas Pacific railroad.

7. Critical Thinking (a) Explain how the growth of the cattle industry was dependent on the development of the railroad industry. (b) Check a modern map of the United States to see which of the mining centers on your map are cities today. Why do you think they have survived?

57   The Spanish-American War

1. Have students use their text or a reference map to locate the places described below. Then have them label each place with its name and the letter of the description.

A. Admiral Dewey destroyed the Spanish fleet in this city's harbor.

B. This city is located at a latitude and longitude of 28° N/82°W.

C. Roosevelt's Rough Riders stormed San Juan hill in the battle over this city.

D. Dewey sailed to the Philippines from this city.

E. Spanish control of this Caribbean island worried the United States since the island was only 90 miles off the coast of Florida.

F. In this city's harbor, a mysterious explosion destroyed the American battleship *Maine*.

G. The latitude and longitude of this city is 24° N/82°W.

2. Ask students to label and locate the following:

Puerto Rico	Florida
Caribbean Sea	Atlantic Ocean
Haiti	Dominican Republic
Philippine Islands	South China Sea
Pacific Ocean	China

3. Have students use different colors or patterns to show the routes of the United States Army and Navy in the Caribbean, the Spanish fleet in the Caribbean, and the United States Navy in the South China Sea during the Spanish-American War.

4. Have them create a key in the blank box.

5. Ask: (a) Where did the United States Navy meet the Spanish fleet in the Caribbean? (b) In which direction did Dewey sail from Hong Kong to the Philippines? (c) What is the approximate latitude and longitude of Puerto Rico? Of Hong Kong? Of Santiago? (d) What strategy did the United States Navy use in the Caribbean?

6. Critical Thinking (a) Check a world map to find out the distance between the Caribbean and the Philippines. What difficulties might there have been in fighting a war in places so far apart? (b) Why did the United States go to war in the Philippines?

58   The United States in the Caribbean, 1898–1917

1. Have students use their text or a reference map to locate and label the following:

United States	Mexico
Guatemala	British Honduras
El Salvador	Nicaragua
Costa Rica	Panama
Cuba	Haiti
Dominican Republic	Puerto Rico
Colombia	Venezuela
Panama Canal Zone	Virgin Islands

Caribbean Sea Pacific Ocean
Gulf of Mexico Atlantic Ocean

2. Ask students to use one color or pattern to shade the areas acquired by the United States and another color or pattern to shade the areas of United States activity between 1898 and 1917.

3. Have them create a key in the blank box.

4. Ask students which of the following statements are supported by the map. Have them correct the incorrect statements.

A. Colombia was under United States influence.
B. The Panama Canal is located on a longitude of approximately 80°W.
C. Honduras was a United States possession.
D. Spain controlled Puerto Rico.
E. The United States owned Panama.
F. Cuba was an area of United States activity.

5. Critical Thinking Defend or refute the following statement: "The proximity of the Caribbean islands and Central America to the United States justified American intervention there." Defend your position with facts.

59 The Panama Canal

1. Have students use their text or a reference map to locate and label the following:

Gatun Lake Colon
Panama City Balboa
Panama Caribbean Sea
Pacific Ocean

2. Ask students to shade the Canal Zone. Then have them use different colors or patterns to show the route ships could take through the canal and the railroad that was built along the canal.

3. Tell students to use a symbol to show the location of the three pairs of locks.

4. Have them create a key in the blank box.

5. Ask: (a) Which bodies of water did the Panama Canal connect? (b) Which city was located at the northern end of the canal? (c) How many miles/kilometers long is the canal? (d) In which direction did ships sail through the canal? (e) What purpose did the locks serve?

6. Critical Thinking (a) What geographical obstacles did the canal-builders face? (b) Check a map of North and South America. What were the benefits of the Panama Canal?

60 Europe in World War I

1. Have students use their text or a reference map to identify the nations described below. Then have them locate and label each nation with its name and the letter of the description.

A. Archduke Francis Ferdinand was assassinated by a man who wanted the unification of Bosnia with this nation.
B. These three nations belonged to the Triple Alliance in 1914.

C. This nation set up a naval blockade and mined the North Sea.
D. A revolution in 1917 forced this nation to leave the war.
E. In 1914, the German army invaded Belgium on its way to this nation.

2. Using their text or a reference map, ask students to locate and label the remainder of the nations outlined on their maps. Have them also locate and label the Atlantic Ocean, the North Sea, the Mediterranean Sea, and the Black Sea.

3. Tell students to use different colors or patterns to shade the Allies and the Central Powers.

4. Have them create a key in the blank box.

5. Ask: (a) Which side did Portugal support in World War I? (b) Which Allied Power was the largest? (c) Which nations had coastlines on the North Sea?

6. Critical Thinking Based on your map, what are the advantages and disadvantages of the geographic location of the Central Powers?

61 The Western Front, 1914–1918

1. Have students use their text or a reference map to locate and label the following:

Germany France
Belgium Netherlands
Luxembourg Brussels
Paris Meuse River
Somme River Marne River
Rhine River

2. Ask students to use lines of different colors or patterns to show (1) how far the German army had advanced by 1914; (2) how far the German army had advanced by 1918; (3) the armistice line of 1918. Then have them draw arrows to show the Allied offensive in 1918.

3. Ask students to locate and label the following battle-sites with a symbol.

Belleau Woods Chateau-Thierry
Reims Ypres
Verdun Meuse-Argonne
Amiens

4. Have them create a key in the blank box.

5. Ask: (a) Which battles took place on the Marne River? (b) When were German troops closest to Paris? (c) In which direction did the Allied offensive push?

6. Critical Thinking Based on the map, during which period of time did the war start to turn in favor of the Allied nations?

62 Europe After World War I

1. Have students use their text or a reference map to locate and label the nations outlined on their maps.

2. Ask students to use different colors or patterns to shade the territories lost by Austria-Hungary, Bulgaria, Germany, and Russia after World War I.

3. Have them create a key in the blank box.

4. Tell students to compare this map to one showing Europe in 1914. Ask students which of the following statements are supported by the information on both maps. Have them correct the incorrect statements.

A. After the war, Portugal gained Morocco as a territory.

B. Russia lost the greatest amount of land after World War I.

C. Bulgaria lost direct access to the Mediterranean.

D. Austria-Hungary became one nation after the war.

E. The newly formed nation of Yugoslavia consisted of the lands that at one time made up Serbia, part of Bulgaria, and part of Austria-Hungary.

F. At the end of World War I, Albania became part of Romania.

G. France gained the territory of Alsace-Lorraine from Germany.

5. **Critical Thinking** Based on your map, how did the Allied Powers try to insure that the former Central Powers would be permanently weakened?

63 Tennessee Valley Authority

1. Have students use their text or a reference map to locate and label the states outlined on their maps. Then ask students to locate and label the following:

Cumberland River	Tennessee River
Mississippi River	Knoxville
Bowling Green	Nashville
Atlanta	Memphis
Chattanooga	Birmingham

2. Tell students to shade the area which received electric power through the Tennessee Valley Authority (TVA).

3. Ask students to use a symbol to show where dams were built.

4. Have them create a key in the blank box.

5. Ask: (a) On which rivers did the TVA build dams? (b) Which states benefited from the electric power provided by the TVA? (c) Which mountain range ran through this area?

6. **Critical Thinking** How did the dams built by the TVA improve the geographic environment for farmers?

64 Aggression in Europe

1. Have students use their text or a reference map to locate the areas described below. Then have them label each area with its name and the letter of the description.

A. This area, located on the border of France and Belgium, was the first to be occupied by the German army.

B. In September 1938, the western part of Czechoslovakia, known by this name, was annexed by Germany.

C. Germany took over this country after the Munich Conference.

D. In the Nazi-Soviet Pact, Germany and the Soviet Union agreed to divide this nation.

E. This nation conquered Albania in 1939.

2. Ask students to use their information source to locate and label the remaining nations outlined on their maps.

3. Have students use different colors or patterns to shade (1) Germany at the end of World War I; (2) the area taken by Germany from 1936 to 1937; (3) the area taken by Germany from 1938 to September 1, 1939; (4) Italy at the end of World War I; (5) the area taken by Italy from 1938 to 1939.

4. Have them create a key in the blank box.

5. Ask (a) During which period of time did Germany take over the most territory? (b) From which nations did Germany take land between 1936 and 1939? (c) Which European country did Italy take over? (d) What is the approximate latitude and longitude of the Rhineland?

6. **Critical Thinking** Based on your map, describe how German and Italian aggression were changing the face of Europe.

65 World War II in Europe and North Africa

1. Have students use their text or a reference map to locate and label the nations outlined on their maps. Then have students locate and label the following:

Casablanca	Tunis
Berlin	El Alamein
Moscow	Dunkirk
Paris	Salerno
Warsaw	Stalingrad
Atlantic Ocean	Black Sea
Mediterranean Sea	North Sea
Baltic Sea	

2. Ask students to use different colors or patterns to shade (1) Allied territory in 1942; (2) the main Axis nations; (3) territory controlled by the Axis in 1942.

3. Have students use lines to show the Allied advances from 1942 to 1945. They should show the advances from the Soviet Union through Eastern Europe, advances from Great Britain, and advances from Africa.

4. Have them create a key in the blank box.

5. Ask students which of the following statements are supported by the map. Have them correct the incorrect statements.

A. Great Britain was under Axis control in 1942.

B. The Allies attacked Italy from Tunis.

C. The Axis Powers had taken over Poland before 1942.

D. The approximate latitude and longitude of Moscow in 55°N/37°E.

E. Yugoslavia remained neutral throughout World War II.

F. Italy was an Allied nation.

G. Allied armies advanced west from the Soviet Union toward Germany.

H. Allied forces crossed the Mediterranean Sea from Africa to Sicily.

6. Critical Thinking Based on your map, describe the strategy used by the Allied Powers to defeat the Axis Powers.

66 World War II in the Pacific

1. Have students use their text or a reference map to locate and label the following:

Tarawa	Wake Island
Guam	New Guinea
Philippine Islands	Leyte Gulf
Japan	Manchuria
Korea	China
Burma	Thailand
French Indochina	Australia
Hawaiian Islands	Midway Island
Iwo Jima	Okinawa

2. Ask students to locate and label the following cities:

Tokyo	Hiroshima
Nagasaki	Hong Kong
Shanghai	Chungking
Manila	

3. Tell students to shade the areas under Japanese control in 1942. Then have them use a dashed line to show the area in Asia and the Pacific under Japanese control in 1942.

4. Have them create a key in the blank box.

5. Ask: (a) Which parts of China were under Japanese control in 1942? (b) At approximately what latitude and longitude is Tokyo? Wake Island? The Hawaiian Islands? (c) Which parts of the United States were most threatened by Japanese expansion?

6. Critical Thinking (a) What geographic features would have made an Allied attack on this area difficult? (b) What geographic features would have made the area difficult for the Japanese to defend?

67 Germany Divided

1. Have students use their text or a reference map to locate and label the countries outlined on their maps.

2. Ask them to use different colors or patterns to shade the areas of Germany occupied by the United States, Great Britain, France, and the Soviet Union. Have them locate and label Berlin as an international zone.

3. Have them create a key in the blank box.

4. Ask students which of the following statements are supported by the map. Have them correct the incorrect statements.

A. Great Britain occupied the northwest section of Germany.

B. Berlin was in the French quarter of Germany.

C. The United States quarter of Germany bordered Austria and Czechoslovakia.

D. The Soviet Union occupied the southwest section of Germany.

E. Poland is east of Germany.

5. Critical Thinking Study a modern map of Germany. Did post-war occupation by the Allied Powers seem to have any lasting effects on Germany? Explain.

68 Europe After World War II

1. Have students use their text or a reference map to locate and label the countries outlined on their maps.

2. Ask them to use different colors or patterns to shade the nations who had joined the North Atlantic Treaty Organization (NATO) and the nations who had joined the Warsaw Pact in 1955.

3. Have students create a key in the blank box.

4. Ask: (a) Which nations belonged to NATO? Which to the Warsaw Pact? (b) Which nations remained neutral? (c) Which Eastern European nations belonged to NATO? (d) At approximately what longitude were East and West Germany divided? (e) Through which countries does the prime meridian run?

5. Critical Thinking (a) What generalization can you make about how post-World War II treaties divided Europe? (b) Which organization did the United States join, NATO or the Warsaw Pact? (c) Why do you think the United States joined a European alliance?

69 The Korean War

1. Have students use their text or a reference map to locate the geographical or historical features described below. Have them draw each feature where required and label it with its name and the letter of the description.

A. After World War II, this parallel divided the country into a northern zone and a southern zone.

B. Soviet troops helped establish a communist government in this country after World War II.

C. This country was invaded by North Korea in 1950.

D. North Korean forces advanced as far as this line in September 1950.

E. United Nations forces advanced as far as this line in November 1950.

F. This river runs along the longest part of the border between North Korea and China.

G. Chinese and North Korean forces together advanced as far as this line in January 1951.

2. Have students create a key in the blank box.

3. Ask: (a) Which parallel divided North and South Korea before and after the Korean War? (b) Which neighboring nation was most concerned about United Nations and United States troops invading North Korea?

4. Critical Thinking (a) Why do you think the United States led the effort against the North Korean invasion of South Korea? (b) What geographical disadvantage did South Korea have?

70 War in Southeast Asia

1. Have students use their text or a reference map to locate and label the following:

China	Vientiane
Cambodia	Hue
Mekong River	Thailand
Saigon	South Vietnam
Dienbienphu	Hanoi
Laos	Phnom Penh
North Vietnam	Gulf of Tonkin
Red River	

2. Ask students to draw a line showing the demilitarized zone between North and South Vietnam and a dotted line indicating the Ho Chi Minh Trail.

3. Ask students which of the following statements are supported by the map. Have them correct the incorrect statements.

A. The Red River empties into the Gulf of Tonkin.
B. The Ho Chi Minh Trail went through Laos and Thailand.
C. Hanoi is a city in South Vietnam.
D. The Mekong River runs along much of the border between Laos and Thailand.
E. The approximate latitude and longitude of Phnom Penh is 11°N/105°E.

4. Critical Thinking (a) Why did the United States support South Vietnam? (b) Why did the United States bomb Cambodia? (c) What effect did the war in Vietnam have on the United States?

71 The World

1. For a period of one week, have students clip and save newspaper articles about United States relations with other nations.

2. At the end of the week, ask students to use their text or a reference map to locate and label all the nations that appear in their articles. Then have them shade the nations they have labeled.

3. Ask: (a) With which nations did the United States interact during the week? (b) What issues were involved? (c) Were the issues primarily political, economic, or social?

4. Critical Thinking How does your map support the idea that the United States is a world power?

72 Western Hemisphere

1. For this lesson, the class will need a population map of the Western Hemisphere and a reference book that tells the Gross National Product (GNP) for the countries listed below.

2. Have students use their text or a reference map to locate, label, and draw the borders of the following places.

United States	Canada
Greenland	Mexico
Nicaragua	El Salvador
Brazil	Haiti
Argentina	Chile

3. Have students make a chart with three columns labeled Nation, Population Density, and GNP. Ask them to fill in the chart for each nation listed above. You may wish to explain to students that population density is the average number of people who live per square mile or per square kilometer. GNP is the total value of all the goods and services produced by the people of a country in one year.

4. Ask students to use one color or pattern to shade nations with a population density of over 512 persons per square mile (over 200 per square kilometer) and another color or pattern to shade nations with a population density of under 512 persons per square mile (under 200 per square kilometer).

5. Have them create a key in the blank box.

6. Ask: (a) Which nation has the greatest population density? (b) What is that nation's GNP? (c) Which nation has the highest GNP?

7. Critical Thinking (a) What relationship can you identify between population density and GNP? (b) How might you explain that relationship?

73 Eastern Hemisphere

1. For this lesson, the class will need a map of the world's mineral resources.

2. Have students use their text or a reference map to locate and label the following continents, countries, and bodies of water. They should draw the borders of any nation listed.

Africa	Australia
Japan	Russia
Saudi Arabia	India
Europe	Atlantic Ocean
Indian Ocean	Arabian Sea
Pacific Ocean	Arctic Ocean
China	South Africa
Iran	

3. Have students use different colors or symbols to indicate areas rich in oil, coal, and uranium. Then ask them to shade the nations that sell these products to the United States.

4. Have them create a key in the blank box.

5. Ask: (a) Which of the above nations has the largest coal fields? (b) Which nations have the largest oil deposits? (c) Which nations sell oil to the United States?

6. Critical Thinking Explain whether the information on your map supports or refutes this statement: "The United States does not depend on other nations for important resources."

74 Africa

1. Have students use their text or a reference map to locate and label the following:

Democratic Republic of Congo   Atlantic Ocean
Zimbabwe   South Africa
Libya   Ethiopia
Somalia   Kenya
Red Sea   Mediterranean Sea
   Indian Ocean

2. Divide students into seven groups and assign each group one of the African nations they labeled in 1.
3. Tell students they will be writing a group report about United States foreign policy in Africa after 1945. Students should use newspaper articles, textbooks, or other sources to find information about the nation their group has been assigned.
4. In their reports, ask students to answer the following questions: (a) Why has the United States been interested in developing a relationship with this nation? (b) Does the nation's geographic location or geographic resources affect its relationship with the United States? (c) What did the United States hope to gain from the relationship? (d) What did the African nation hope to gain?
5. **Critical Thinking** How did each of the following affect United States foreign policy toward the African nation your group researched: economic factors, political factors, social factors, geographic factors?

75 Asia

1. Point out to students that the United States imports a variety of consumer goods from Asian countries. Have students look at advertisements, in stores, and in their homes for products that come from Asian nations.
2. Ask students to make a list of the countries and the products each one exports to the United States.
3. Have students locate and label the nations on their maps. Then have them create a symbol for each product on the list and place the symbols on the countries that export these items to the United States.
4. Have them create a key in the blank box.
5. Ask: (a) What kinds of products does the United States buy from Asian nations? (b) Are there nations for which you did not find products in the United States?
6. **Critical Thinking** Have students find out about United States trade restrictions on Asian nations. Use *The Readers' Guide to Periodical Literature* and a newspaper index to find recent articles. (a) How does the United States restrict trade? (b) Why does it restrict trade?

76 East Asia

1. Have students read about United States and European involvement in East Asia from 1898 to 1914 in their text or a reference book.

2. Have students use their text or a reference map to locate and label the following places. Point out that their outline maps represent present-day national boundaries of East Asian nations. Students may have to redraw boundaries.

Manchuria   New Guinea
Korea   Hong Kong
China   Macao
Siam   Outer Mongolia
Borneo   Sakhalin
Shanghai   Indochina
East Indies   Malay States
Russia   Chungking
Japan   Yangtze River
Burma   Formosa
Philippine Islands

3. Ask students to use different colors or patterns to show possessions or areas of influence of Britain, France, Germany, Japan, Portugal, the United States, the Netherlands, and Russia from 1898 to 1914.
4. Have them create a key in the blank box.
5. Ask students which of the following statements are supported by the map. Have them correct the incorrect statements.

A. Korea was under Japanese influence.
B. Indochina was under British control.
C. Formosa was under Japanese control.
D. Russia controlled Manchuria and Outer Mongolia.
E. The British controlled the cities of Chungking, Shanghai, and Hong Kong.
F. A German sphere of influence developed along the Yangtze River.
G. The Philippines were claimed by the United States.
H. Most of the East Indies was claimed by the French.

6. **Critical Thinking** (a) How would you explain the geographical location of foreign claims in East Asia and Southeast Asia? (b) Why was the United States involved in this region?

77 Europe

1. Have students use their text or a reference map to locate and label the countries outlined on their maps.
2. Ask students to find out what type of currency each of the following countries uses. Then have them label the country with the name of the currency.

England   Germany
France   Italy
Spain   Switzerland

3. Point out to students that the value of all currencies, including the American dollar, does not remain constant. The value of currencies changes due to a variety of political and economic factors.
4. Have students use a daily newspaper to find the exchange rates for the currencies of the countries listed in 2. Ask them to make a chart with two columns and six rows. Have students label the columns Foreign Currency in Dollars and Dollar in Foreign Currency; have

them label the rows with the names of the countries listed above. In the first column they should put how many American dollars one unit of the foreign currency will buy and in the second column how many units of the foreign currency one American dollar will buy.

5. Ask: (a) Which currency buys the largest amount of American dollars? (b) How many British pounds does the American dollar buy?

6. **Critical Thinking** Explain how the exchange rate is used in each of the following situations.

A. An American businesswoman is traveling to France.
B. A buyer for an English department store is going to purchase shoes from a manufacturer in Italy.
C. A French bank wants to decide whether it should invest its money in currency from Spain, England, or the United States.
D. You are planning a trip to Switzerland and need to decide how much hotels and meals will cost you in American dollars.

78   Middle East

1. Have students use their text or a reference map to locate and label the following places. For this lesson, the class will also need a map of the world's oil resources.

Turkey	Iran
Syria	Iraq
Cyprus	Lebanon
Israel	Jordan
Kuwait	Egypt
Yemen	P.D.R. of Yemen
Oman	Bahrain
Qatar	United Arab Emirates
Red Sea	Mediterranean Sea
Persian Gulf	Saudi Arabia

2. Ask students to create a symbol to represent oil. Then have them use the symbol to designate where oil is located in the Middle East.

3. Have them create a key in the blank box.

4. Have students find out which countries around the world sell oil to the United States. Then ask them to make a chart listing the percentage of its oil imports the United States buys from each nation.

5. Ask: (a) From which region of the world does the United States buy most of its oil? (b) From which part of the world does the United States purchase the least oil?

6. **Critical Thinking** What role do you think geography and politics play in determining where the United States buys oil? Explain.

79   North America

1. Have students use their text or a reference map to locate and label the following:

United States	Mexico
Guatemala	El Salvador
Honduras	Nicaragua
Costa Rica	Panama
Cuba	Belize
Canada	Greenland
Caribbean Sea	Atlantic Ocean
Pacific Ocean	Jamaica

2. Ask students which of the following statements are supported by the map. Have them correct the incorrect statements.

A. In the Caribbean, Jamaica is the nation nearest to the United States.
B. Guatemala shares a border with Mexico.
C. El Salvador is located on the Pacific Ocean.
D. Panama is directly south of Nicaragua.
E. Honduras is directly north of Nicaragua.
F. Costa Rica borders both the Atlantic and Pacific oceans.

3. **Critical Thinking** (a) How has the geography of the Central American nations affected their economies? (b) What role has the United States played in the economies of these countries?

80   South America

1. Have students use their text or a reference map to locate and label the countries outlined on their maps.

2. Students will need a reference map of South American economic activities. Ask them to use different colors or symbols to indicate the countries where the following industries flourish: oil, coffee, sugar cane, and cacao.

3. Have them create a key in the blank box.

4. Have students find out which nations export these goods to the United States.

5. Ask: (a) Which nations produce coffee? (b) From which nations does the United States buy oil?

6. **Critical Thinking** How do you think geography affects the economies of South American nations?

81   Central America and the Caribbean

1. Have students use their text or a reference map to locate and label the following:

Guatemala	Honduras
Belize	El Salvador
Nicaragua	Costa Rica
Panama	Cuba
Haiti	Dominican Republic
Jamaica	Puerto Rico
Gulf of Mexico	Caribbean Sea

2. For a period of one week, ask students to clip and save newspaper articles about the United States and the nations labeled in 1.

3. Have students shade all the nations that appear in their articles.

4. Have them create a key in the blank box.

5. Ask: (a) Which nations did the United States interact with during the week? (b) What issues were involved?

6. **Critical Thinking** Why do you think the United States is involved in the affairs of the nations of this region?

82 Political United States

1. Have students use their text or a reference map to locate and label the 50 states.

2. Ask students to use two different symbols to indicate each state's capital city and its most populated city. Have them label the cities. In some cases they will be the same city, and in other cases they will not.

3. Have them create a key in the blank box.

4. Ask each student to choose a different state and find out why the capital city is or is not the largest city. They should find out how the particular location of the state capital was chosen and how factors like the geographic location and industry of the city affected its growth.

5. After they have completed their research, have students present their findings. You may wish to list on the chalkboard the factors students have found that contribute to large populations.

6. **Critical Thinking** Make a generalization about factors that contribute to the size of a city.

83 Physical United States

1. Have students use their text or a reference map to locate and label the following:

Rocky Mountains	Appalachian Mountains
Mississippi River	St. Lawrence River
Snake River	Ohio River
Great Lakes	Rio Grande
Colorado River	Missouri River

2. Point out to students that after the American Revolution, the United States settled the North American continent in a general pattern moving from east to west. Ask students to use a reference map which shows the patterns of settlement from about 1790 to 1890.

3. Have students use different colors or patterns to shade the areas that were settled during the following periods: (1) before 1790; (2) from 1790 to 1830; (3) from 1830 to 1870; (4) from 1870 to 1890.

4. Have them create a key in the blank box.

5. Ask students which of the following statements are supported by the map. Have them correct the incorrect statements.

A. By 1790, the United States had been settled up to the Rocky Mountains.

B. Americans had settled on the Pacific Coast by 1870.

C. The Mississippi River empties into the Gulf of Mexico at a longitude of about 90°W.

D. Settlers may have traveled through the northwest region of the United States on the Mississippi and Ohio rivers.

E. The area of the Rocky Mountains remained sparsely populated through 1890.

F. The Rio Grande forms part of the boundary between the United States and Mexico.

G. The area around the Ohio River was settled after 1870.

6. **Critical Thinking** Describe how physical geography affected patterns of settlement during the United States' first hundred years.

84 Eastern United States

1. Have students use their text or a reference map to locate and label the states outlined on their maps. Then have them locate and label the following:

Appalachian Mountains	Lake Ontario
Lake Erie	Lake Huron
Lake Michigan	Lake Superior
Mississippi River	Ohio River
St. Lawrence River	Hudson River
Tennessee River	

2. Ask students to locate the following cities. Then have them find out the population of each one. Ask them to use different symbols to label cities with populations of over 3 million, between 1 million and 3 million, and between 500,000 and 1 million.

New York, New York
Washington, D.C.
Indianapolis, Indiana
Baltimore, Maryland
Detroit, Michigan
Milwaukee, Wisconsin
Philadelphia, Pennsylvania
Jacksonville, Florida
Chicago, Illinois
New Orleans, Louisiana
Boston, Massachusetts
Columbus, Ohio
Memphis, Tennessee

3. Have them create a key in the blank box.

4. Ask: (a) On which lake is the city of Milwaukee located? (b) What is the latitude and longitude of Jacksonville? Of Indianapolis? (c) Which cities have direct access to the Atlantic Ocean? (d) What is the population of Boston?

5. **Critical Thinking** The cities you have labeled on your outline map are the largest ones east of the Mississippi River. Study the map and make a generalization about the geographic location of these cities.

85 Western United States

1. Have students use their text or a reference map to locate and label the states outlined on their maps. Then ask students to locate the places described below and label each one with its name and the letter of its description.

A. This mountain range runs from Alaska to Mexico.
B. The border between Texas and Mexico is defined by this river.
C. This river begins in the state of Minnesota and empties into the Gulf of Mexico.
D. This river is the major tributary of the Mississippi River.
E. This lake is the largest salt water lake in the Western Hemisphere.

2. Tell students to locate and label the Columbia, Snake, Colorado, and Arkansas rivers.

3. Ask students to find a map showing how western lands are used. Then have them use different colors or patterns to shade land used for grazing, dairy cattle and hay, wheat, livestock and feed grains, fruits and vegetables, and general farming.

4. Have them create a key in the blank box.

5. Ask: (a) In which states are fruits and vegetables grown? (b) Where is wheat grown? (c) How is the land used in Texas? In South Dakota?

6. Critical Thinking How do you think geography affects the way of life in western United States?

86 New England States

1. Have students use their text or a reference map to locate the places described below. Then have them label each place with its name and the letter of the description.

A. This state shares a border with only one other state.
B. This state is the smallest one in New England.
C. The hooked peninsula extending from this state was probably named for the abundance of cod fish found there.
D. These two states are separated from each other by the Connecticut River.
E. This state has access to the Atlantic Ocean through the Long Island Sound.

2. Ask students to locate and label the following places. Have them use different symbols to differentiate between state capitals and other cities.

Green Mountains
Connecticut River
Boston, Massachusetts
Concord, New Hampshire
Hartford, Connecticut
Merrimac River
New Haven, Connecticut
Penobscot River
Kennebec River
St. Lawrence River
Cape Cod
Augusta, Maine
Providence, Rhode Island
Portland, Maine
Springfield, Massachusetts
Lake Champlain
Burlington, Vermont
Montpelier, Vermont

3. Have them create a key in the blank box.

4. Ask: (a) In which direction does the Connecticut River flow? (b) What is the latitude and longitude of Boston? Of New Haven?

5. Critical Thinking What are the advantages and disadvantages of direct access to the Atlantic Ocean for the New England states?

87 Middle Atlantic States

1. Have students use their text or a reference map to locate and label the states outlined on their maps. Then ask students to locate and label the following places. Tell them to use a symbol to designate the capital of each state.

Long Island, New York
New York, New York
Baltimore, Maryland
Washington, D.C.
Annapolis, Maryland
Delaware River
Ohio River
Adirondack Mountains
Lake Champlain
Hudson River
Pittsburgh, Pennsylvania
Philadelphia, Pennsylvania
Dover, Delaware
Harrisburg, Pennsylvania
Allegheny River
Albany, New York
Appalachian Mountains
Lake Ontario

2. Ask students to use a reference map to find out where the following modern industries are located in the Middle Atlantic states: iron and steel works, chemicals, textiles, furniture, and petroleum and coal products. Then have students use a different symbol to label where each of these industries is located.

3. Have them create a key in the blank box.

4. Ask students which of the following statements are supported by the map. Have them correct the incorrect statements.

A. There are iron and steel works in Pennsylvania.
B. New Jersey is south of Delaware.
C. New York does not have a textile industry.
D. The furniture industry is spread throughout the Middle Atlantic states.
E. The latitude and longitude of Harrisburg is 38°N/79°W.
F. New York City is the capital of New York state.
G. The Allegheny River runs through Pennsylvania.

5. Critical Thinking (a) Why do you think rivers, lakes, and mountains were important in the early industrial development of the Middle Atlantic states? (b) Do you think they are as important today? Explain.

88 Southeastern States

1. Have students use their text or a reference map to locate and label the states outlined on their maps. Then have students locate and label the capital city of each state.

2. Ask students to locate and label the following places:

Mississippi River	Savannah River
Roanoke River	Tennessee River
Lake Okeechobee	Florida Everglades
Appalachian Mountains	

3. Have students use a reference map to locate the places where the following agricultural activities take place: cattle and hogs, tobacco, fruits and vegetables, cotton, and sugar cane. Ask students to create symbols to represent each of these agricultural products. Then have them label the places where these agricultural industries are located.

4. Have them create a key in the blank box.

5. Ask: (a) In which states are fruits and vegetables grown? (b) In which states is cotton grown? (c) What agricultural products are raised in South Carolina?

6. Critical Thinking How do you think farmers in the Southeastern states are affected by geography?

89 North Central States

1. Have students use their text or a reference map to locate and label the states outlined on their maps. Then have them locate and label the following:

Lake Superior	Lake Michigan
Lake Huron	Lake Erie
Mississippi River	Ohio River
Missouri River	

2. Ask students to locate and label the capital city of each North Central state.

3. Have students create a symbol for each of the following industries: furniture, iron and steel works, lumber, petroleum and coal products, and chemicals. Ask students to use a reference map and their symbols to label where these industries are located.

4. Have them create a key in the blank box.

5. Ask: (a) What is the latitude and longitude of Pierre, South Dakota? Of Des Moines, Iowa? (b) Which industries exist in Indiana? (c) In which states does the furniture industry exist?

6. Critical Thinking (a) Are there more industries located east or west of the Mississippi River? (b) How do you think geography contributes to the location of industries? (c) Based on your map, make a generalization about the location of industries in the North Central states.

90 South Central States

1. Have students use their text or a reference map to locate and label the following:

Texas	Louisiana
Oklahoma	Arkansas
Little Rock	Baton Rouge
New Orleans	Austin
Dallas	Houston
Oklahoma City	Pecos River
Rio Grande	Red River
Gulf of Mexico	Ouachita Mountains
Brazos River	Mississippi River

2. Ask students to use a mineral resources map to find out where the following are located: oil, magnesium, natural gas, and coal. Then have them use different symbols to label the locations of each mineral resource.

3. Have them create a key in the blank box.

4. Ask students which of the following statements are supported by the map. Have them correct the incorrect statements.

A. Arkansas has direct access to the Gulf of Mexico.
B. There are coal deposits in Texas.
C. Oklahoma does not have any oil reserves.
D. Magnesium is the most abundant mineral resource in the South Central states.
E. The latitude and longitude of Dallas is 33 °N/97 °W.

5. Critical Thinking (a) Which mineral resource is most abundant? (b) How do you think this mineral affects the economy of the South Central states?

91 Rocky Mountain States

1. Have students use their text or a reference map to locate and label the states outlined on their maps. Then have them locate each state's capital city and label it with a symbol.

2. Ask students to locate and label the following:

Rocky Mountains	Snake River
Rio Grande	Great Salt Lake
Missouri River	Colorado River
Gila River	

3. Have students use a map which shows the length of growing seasons. Ask them to use different colors or patterns to shade the areas with growing seasons which last from 9 to 12 months, 7 to 9 months, 5 to 7 months, 3 to 5 months, and less than 3 months.

4. Have them create a key in the blank box.

5. Ask: (a) Through which states does the Colorado River run? (b) What is the capital city of Idaho? (c) Which states have the shortest growing season? (d) Which states have the longest growing season?

6. Critical Thinking (a) How do the Rocky Mountains seem to affect climate? (b) How do you think the Rocky Mountains affect daily life in the states outlined on your map?

92 Pacific Coast States

1. Have students use their text or a reference map to locate the states described below. Then have them label each state with its name and the letter of the description.

A. This state's eastern boundary is defined by the Sierra Nevada.
B. This state is comprised of islands in the Pacific Ocean.
C. When the territory for this state was purchased in 1867, it was called "Seward's Folly" because people thought the land was worthless.
D. The northern boundary of this state lies on the 49th parallel.
E. The southern portion of the Cascade Range falls in this state.

2. Ask students to locate and label the following:

Sierra Nevada	Cascade Range
Rocky Mountains	Columbia River
Snake River	Coast Ranges
Alaska Range	Brooks Range
Juneau	Sacramento
Salem	Olympia
Honolulu	Mohave Desert

3. Have students find out the number of representatives each Pacific Coast state sends to Congress. Then have them find out how representation has changed since the last census due to reapportionment.

4. Ask them to make a chart with two columns labeled Number of Representatives and Change in Representation and one row for each Pacific Coast state.

5. After students fill in their charts, have them use different colors or patterns to shade the states that gained representatives, states that lost representatives, and states that had no change in representation.

6. Have them create a key in the blank box.

7. Ask: (a) Which states gained representation in Congress due to reapportionment? Which states lost representation? (b) At about what latitude and longitude is Olympia? (c) For which states does the Columbia River form a boundary?

8. Critical Thinking (a) Why do states gain or lose representation in Congress? (b) How does representation in Congress affect a state?

1 Hunters Reach America

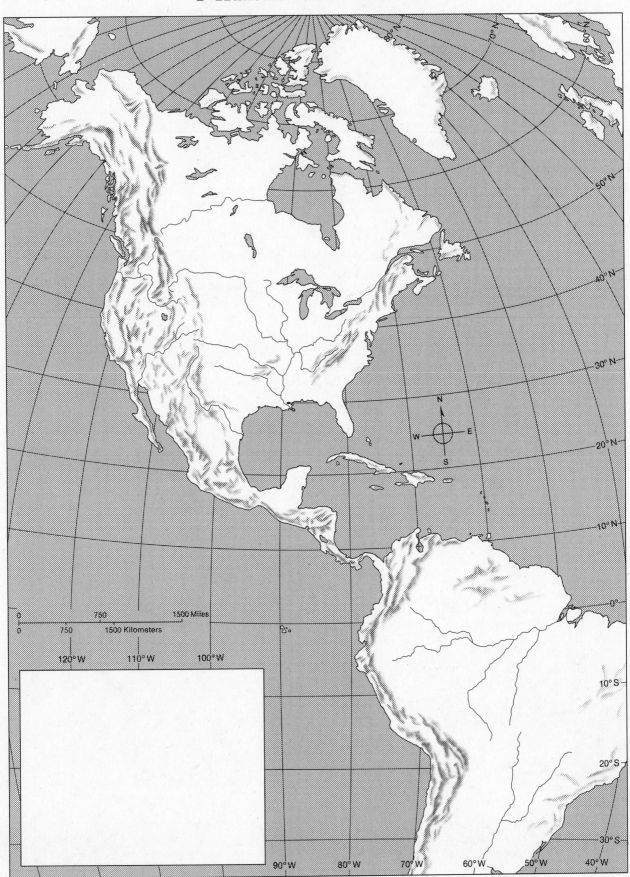

2 Physical Regions of the United States

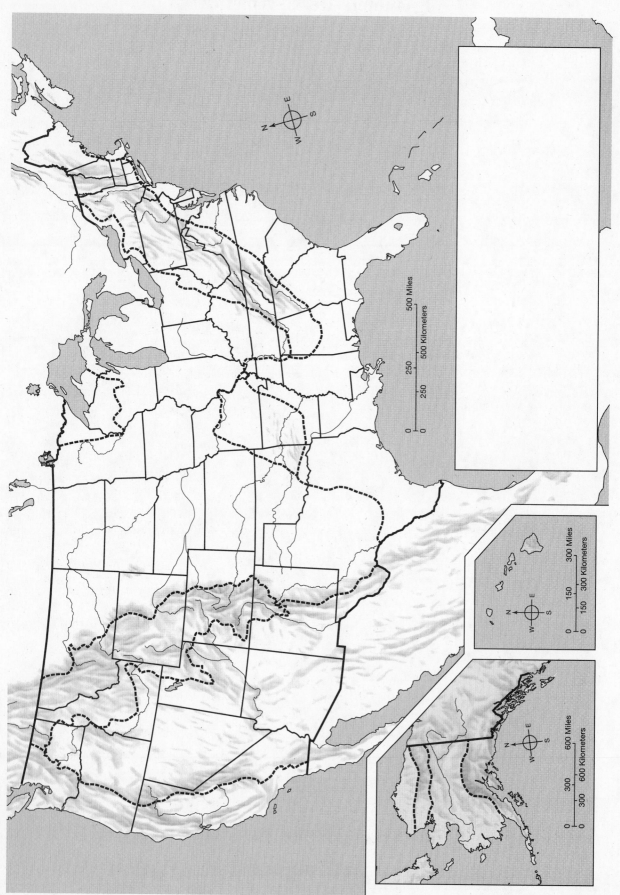

3 Climates of the United States

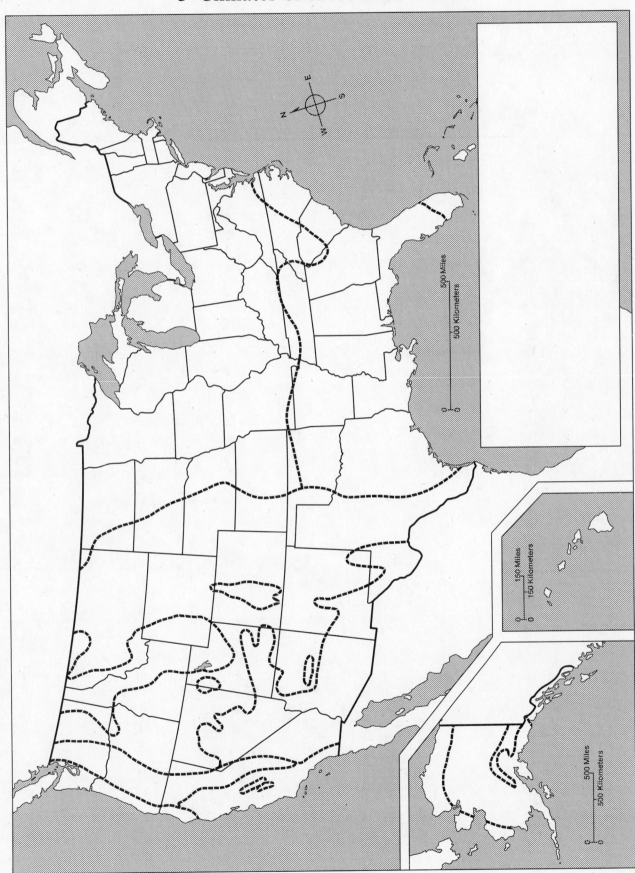

500 Miles

500 Kilometers

150 Miles

150 Kilometers

500 Miles

500 Kilometers

4 Native American Cultures

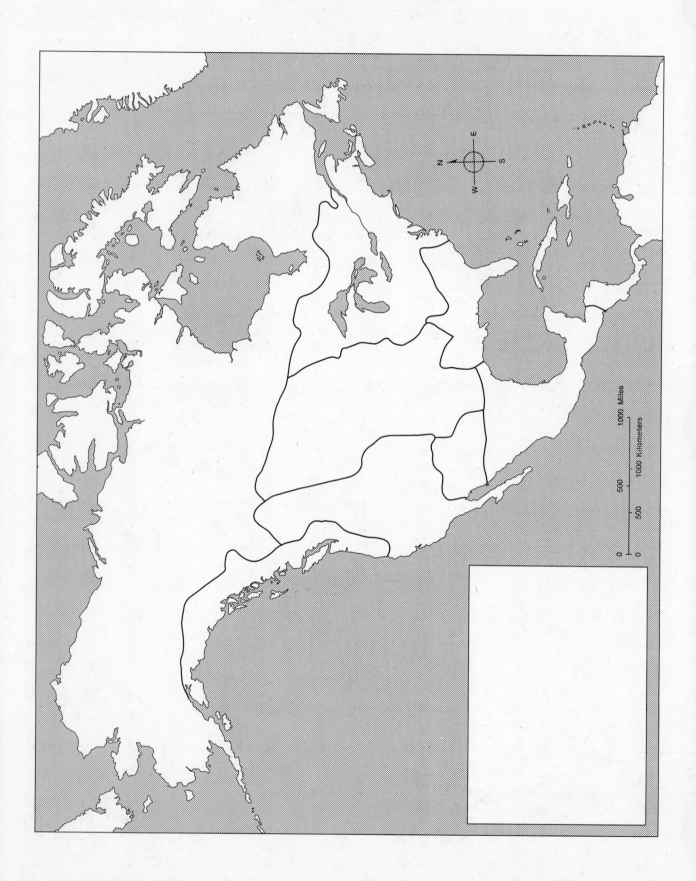

5 Great Empires of the Americas

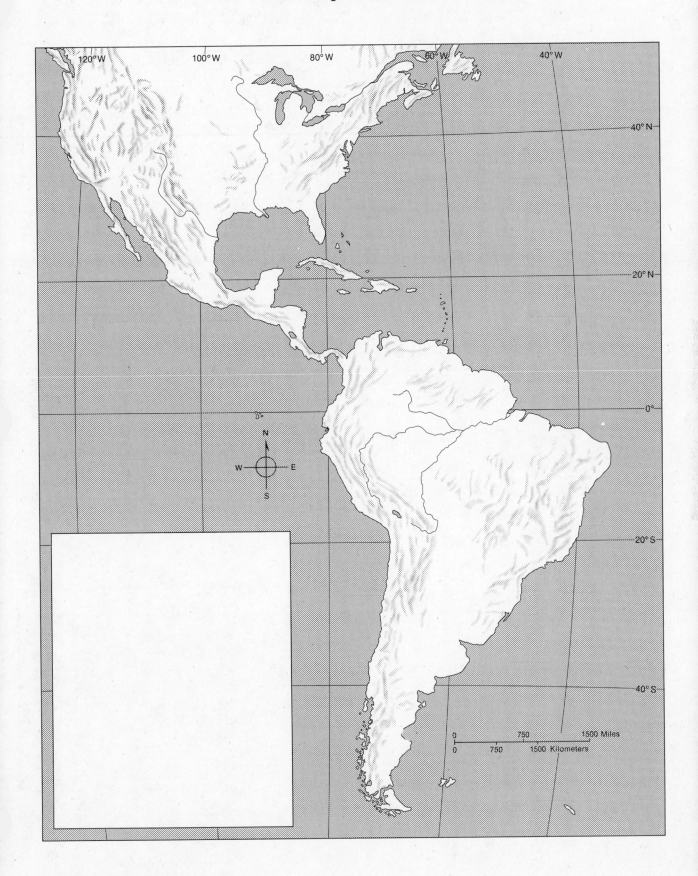

6 To India by Sea

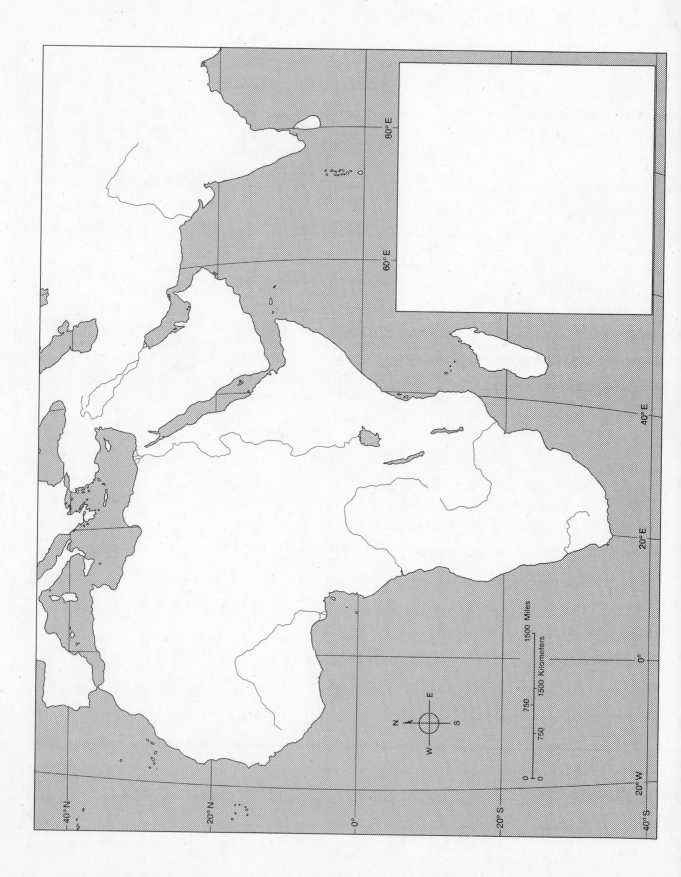

7 Columbus Reaches America

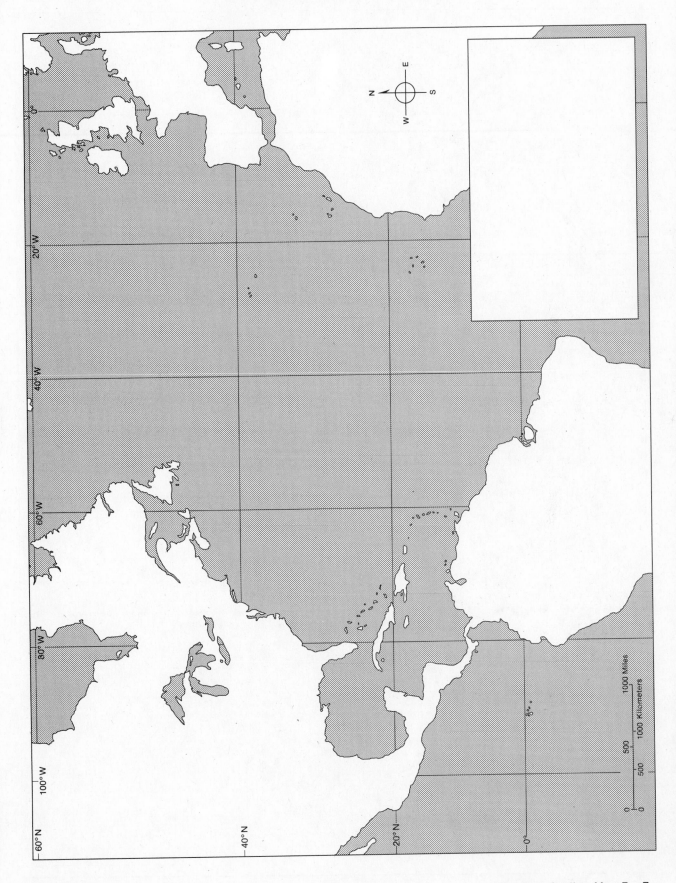

8 Voyages of Discovery

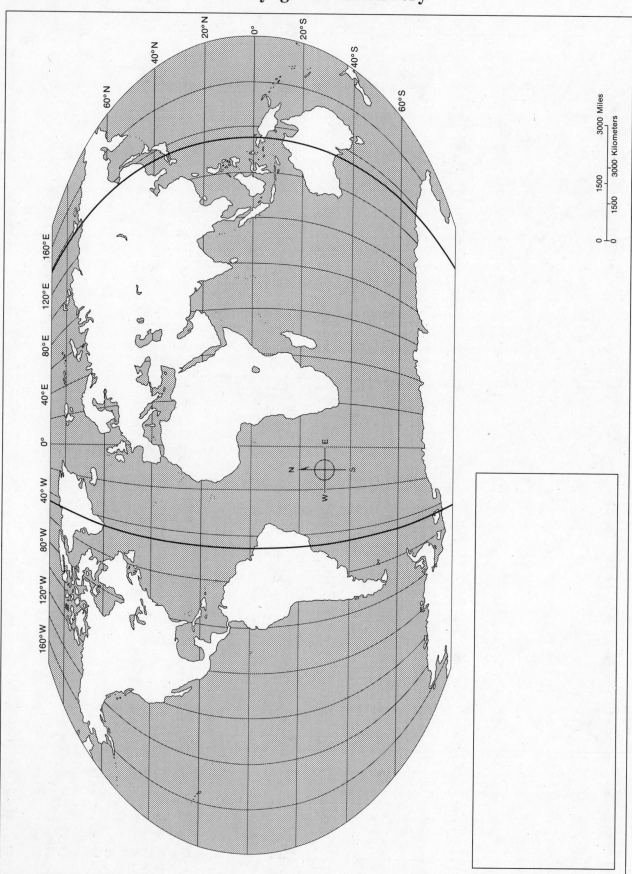

© Prentice-Hall, Inc.

9 Spanish Explorers in North America

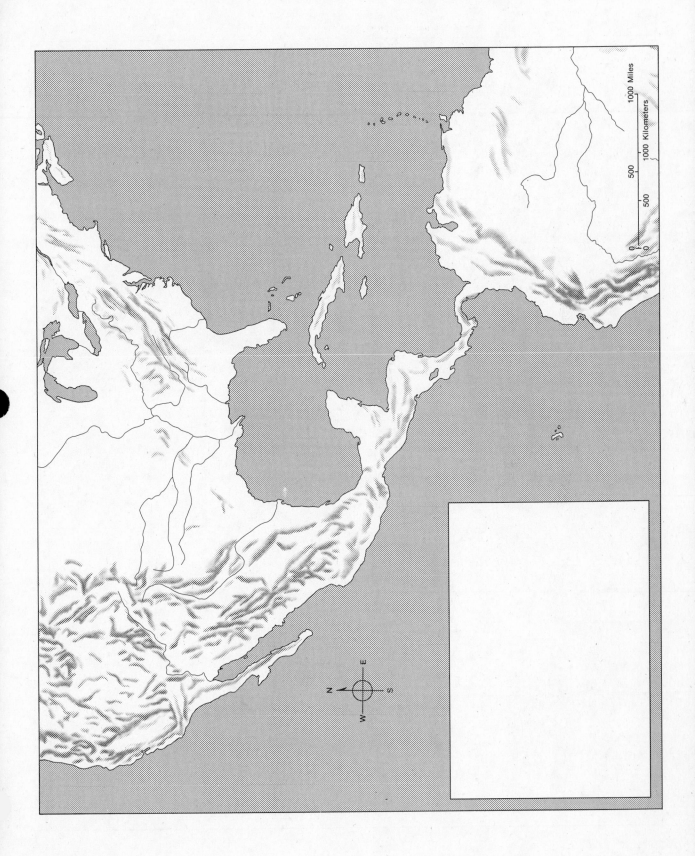

10 Search for a Northwest Passage

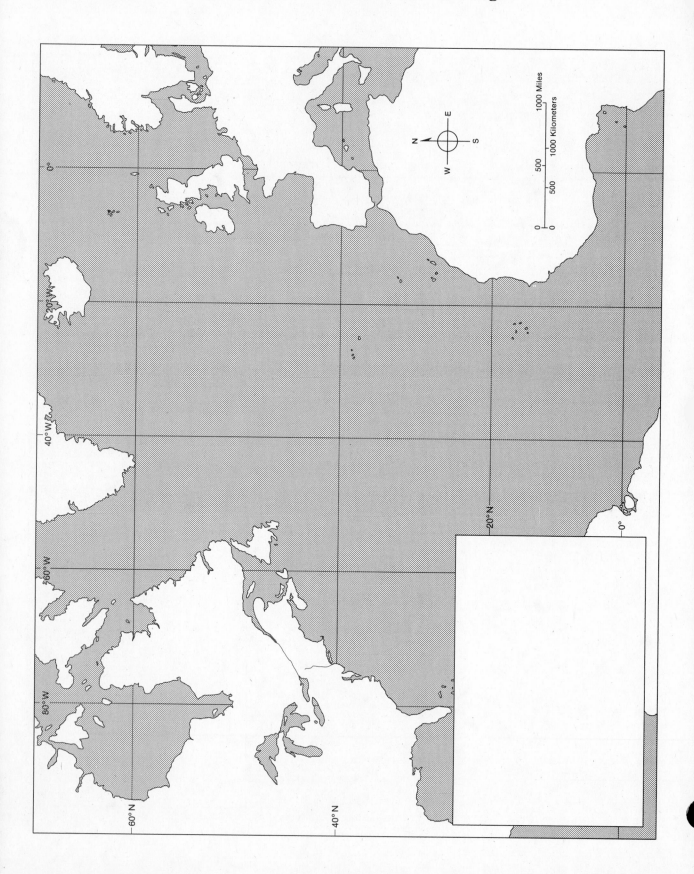

11 Spain and Portugal in the Americas

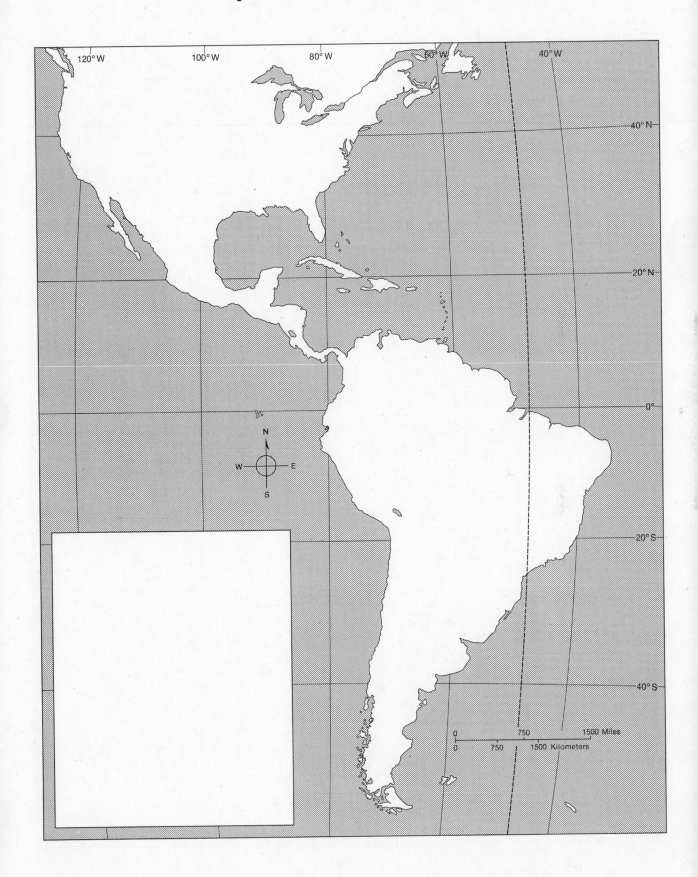

12 The French Explore North America

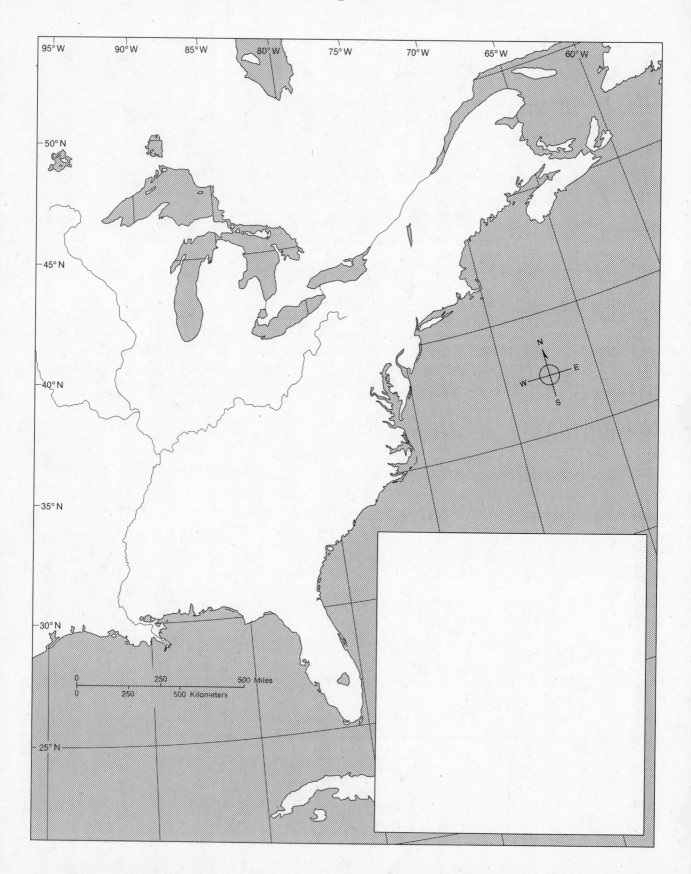

13 New Netherland and New Sweden

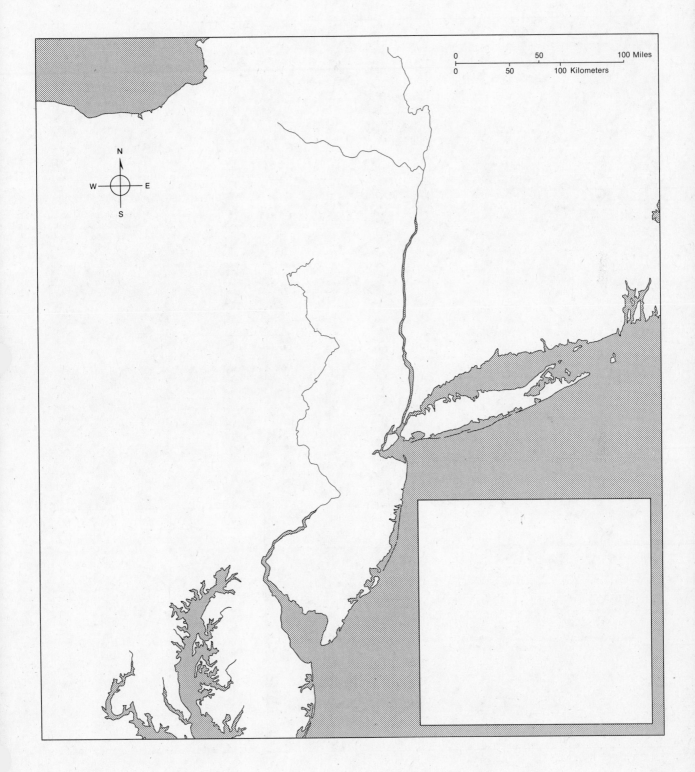

14 The First English Settlements

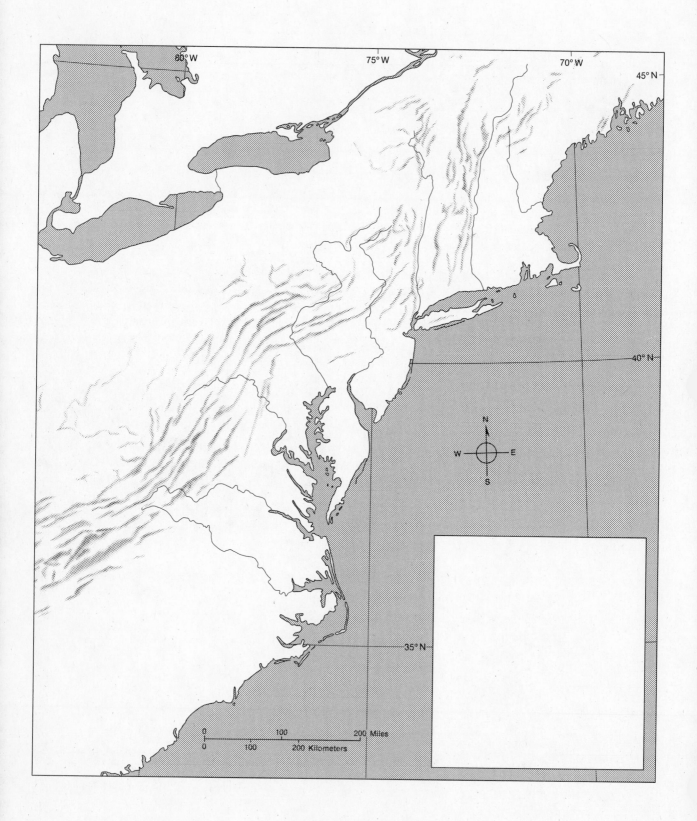

15 The Thirteen Colonies

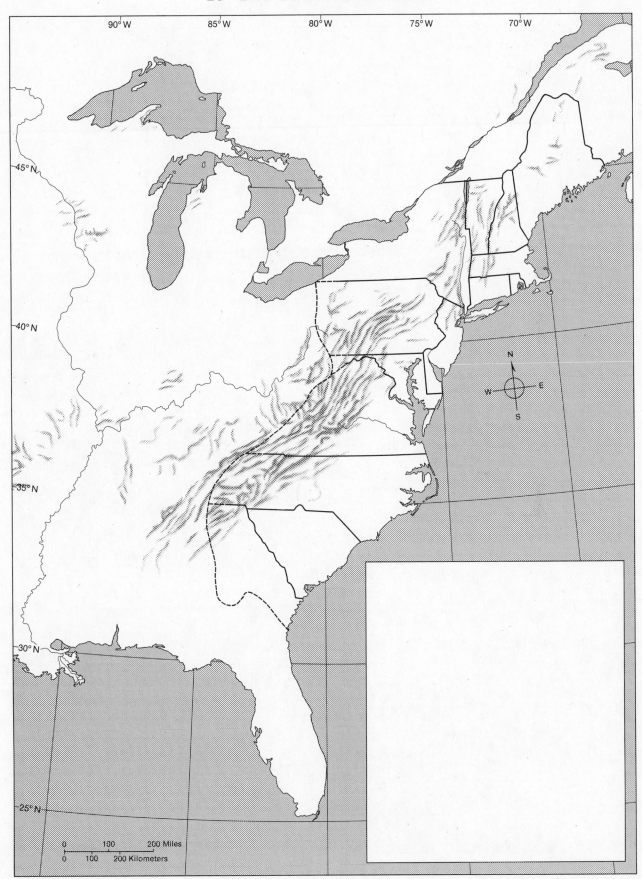

16 The New England Colonies

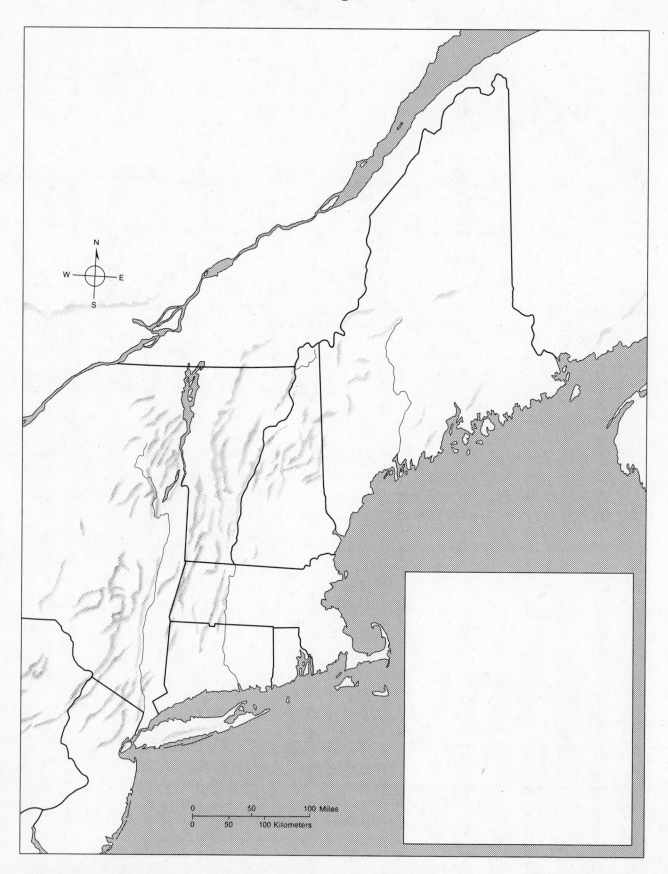

17 The Middle Colonies

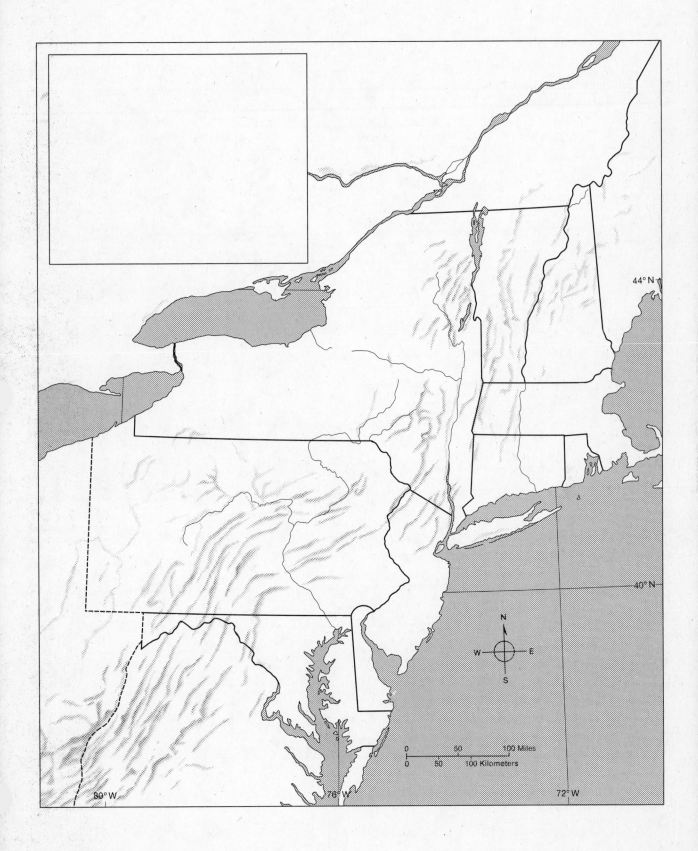

44° N

40° N

N
W   E
S

0		50		100 Miles

0	50	100 Kilometers

80° W

76° W

72° W

18 The Southern Colonies

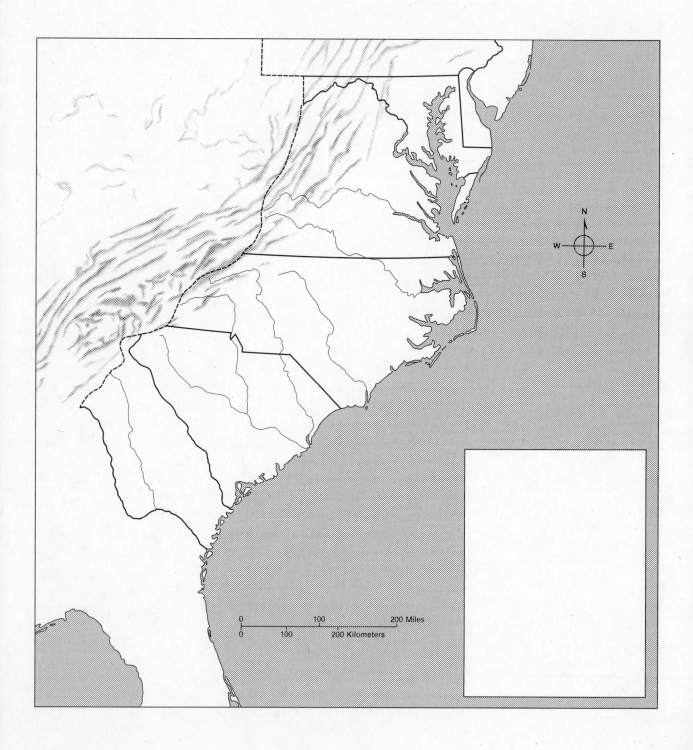

0   100   200 Miles
0   100   200 Kilometers

19 Major Trade Routes

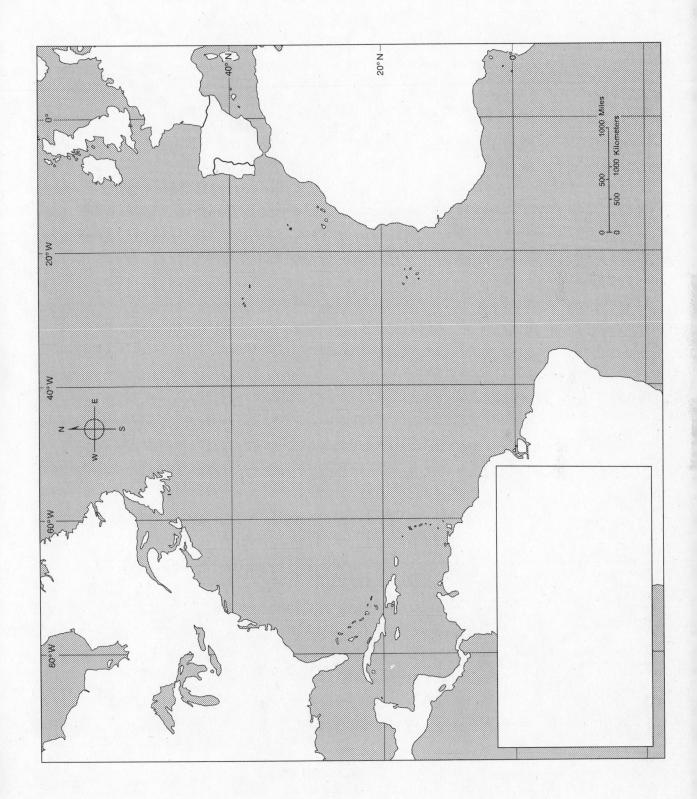

20 North America in 1753

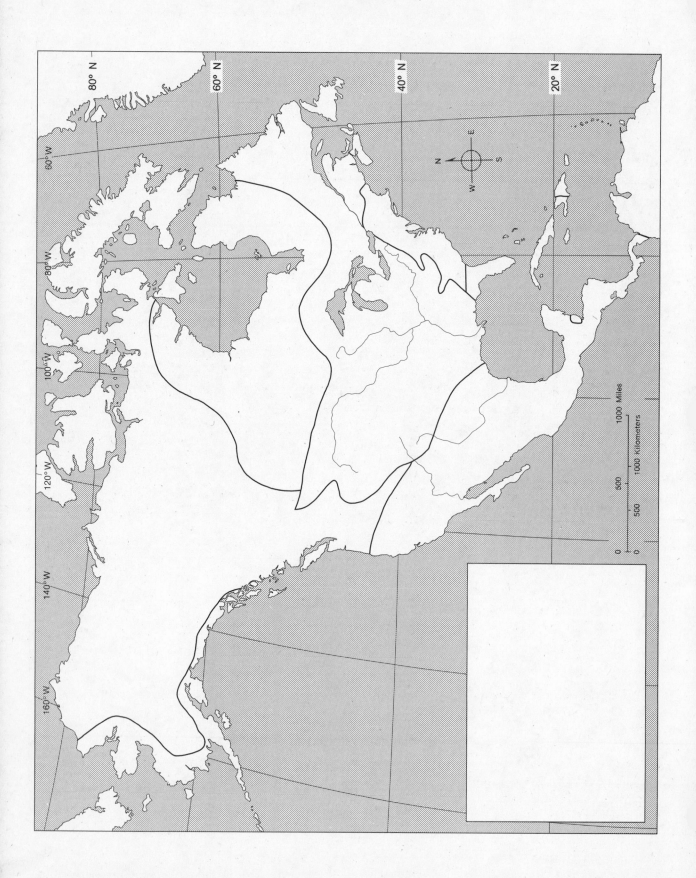

21 The French and Indian War

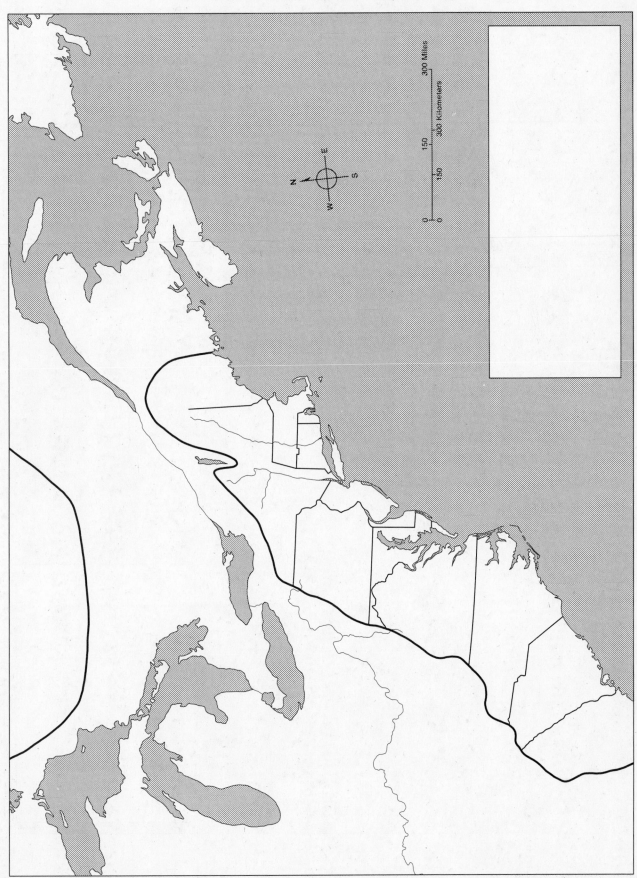

22 North America in 1763

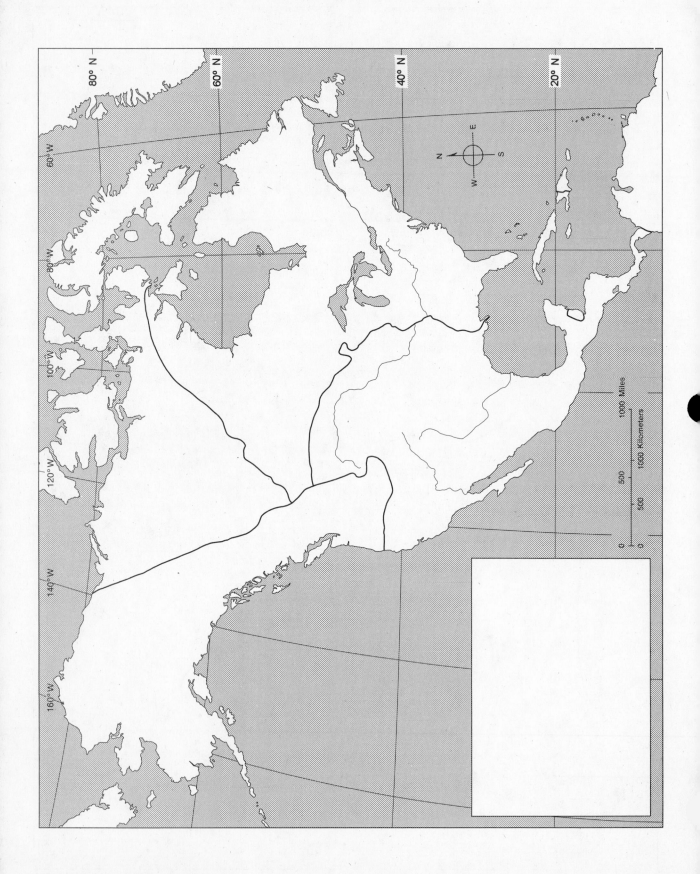

23 Lexington and Concord

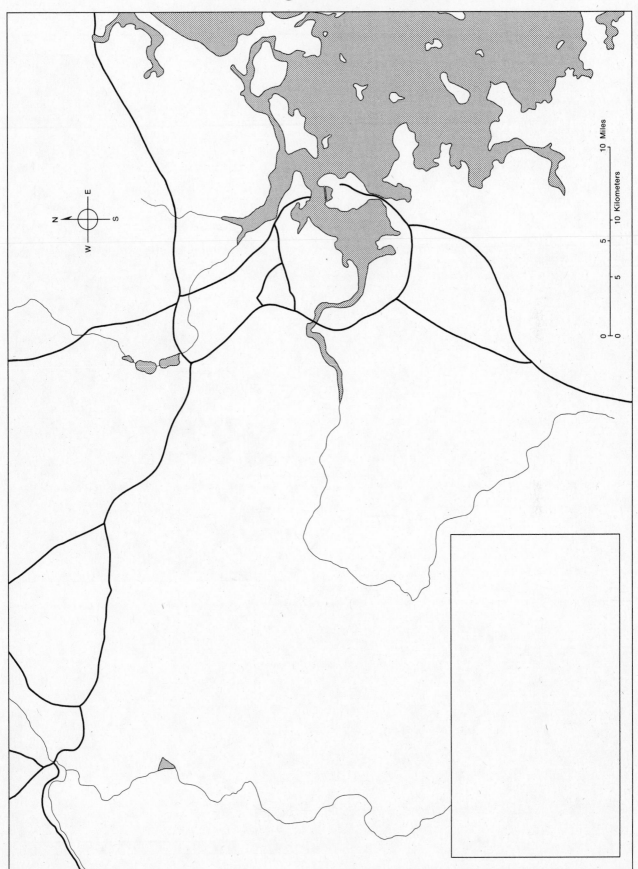

24 The Revolutionary War: An Overview

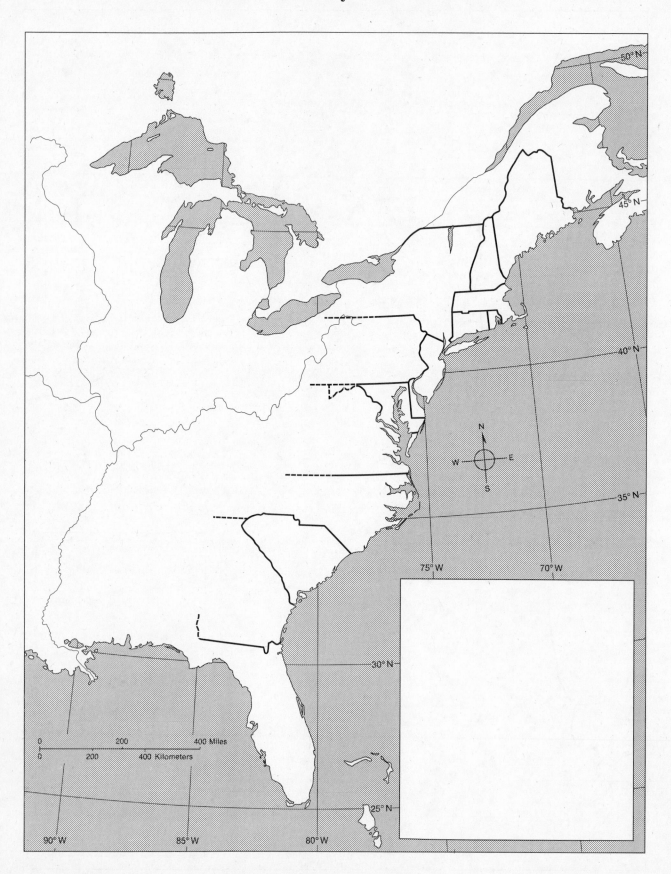

25 The Revolutionary War in the Northeast

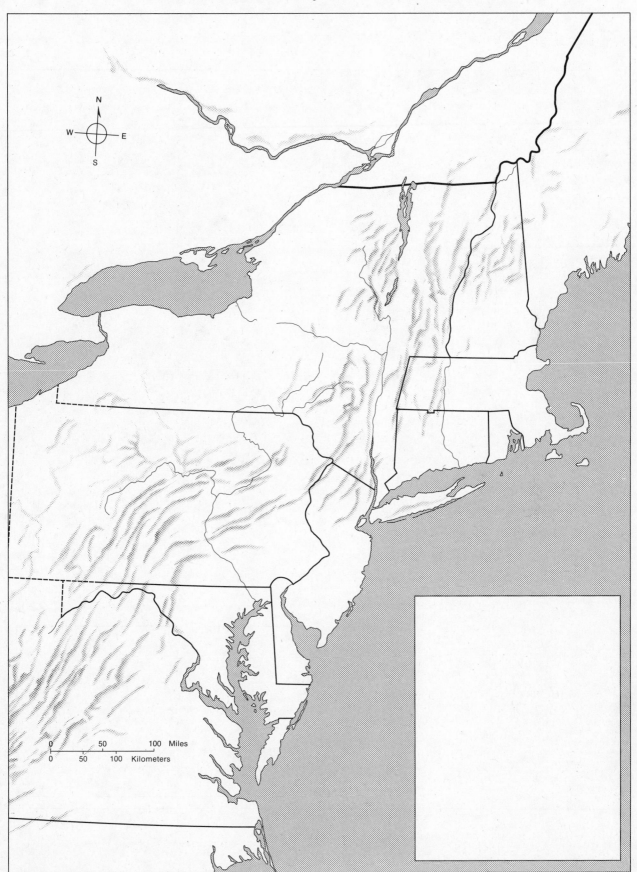

26 The Revolutionary War in the West

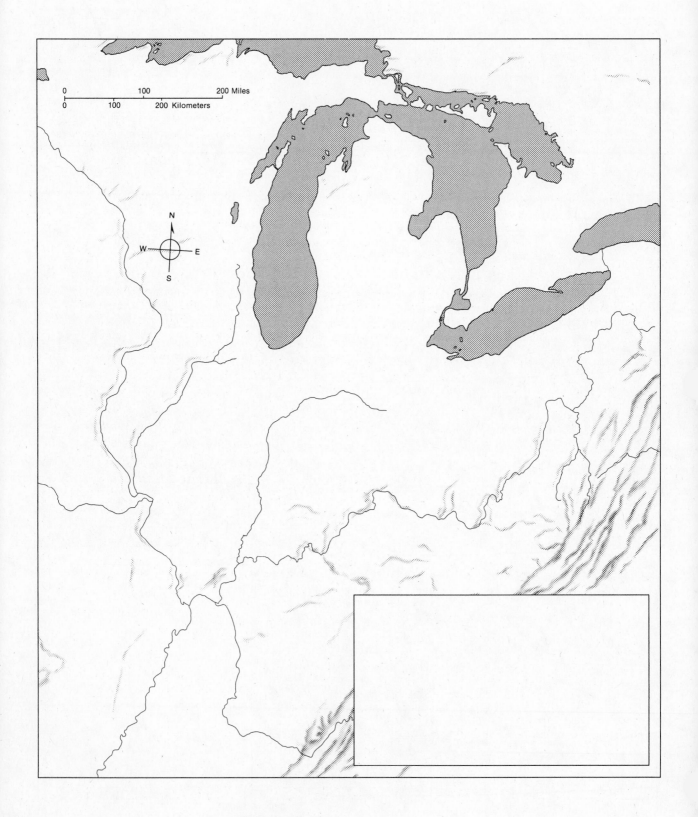

27 The Revolutionary War in the South

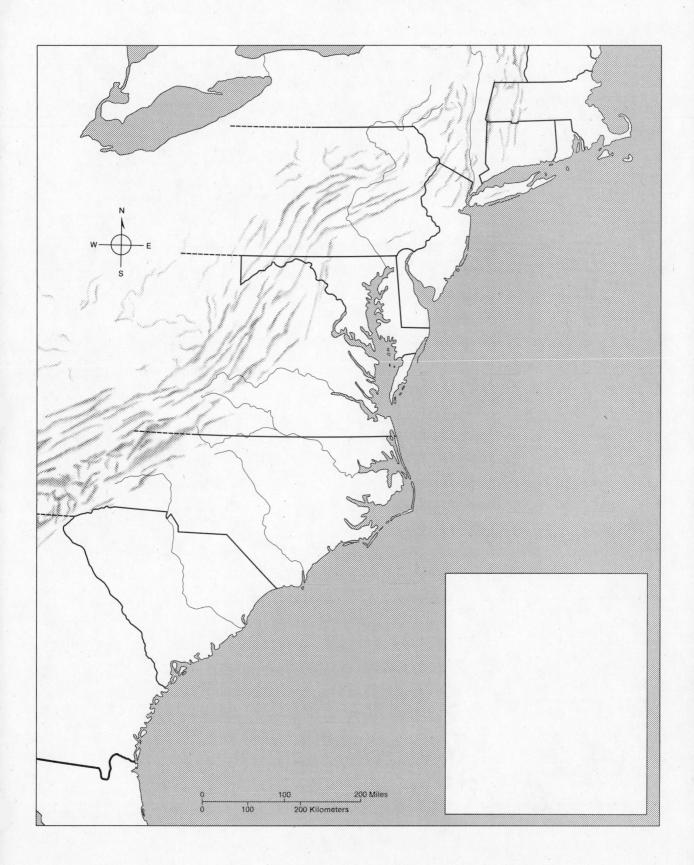

28 North America in 1783

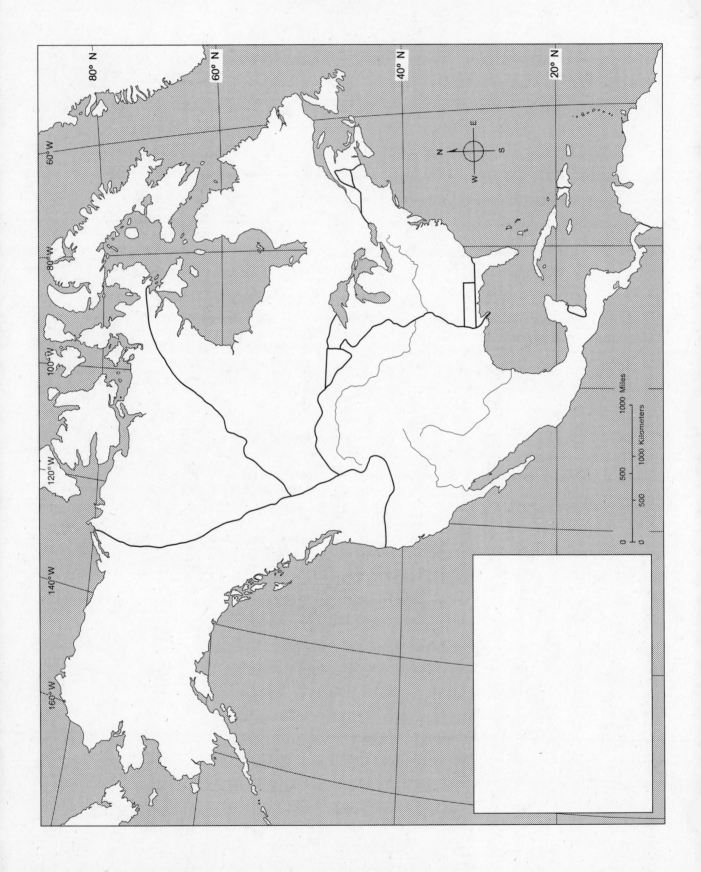

29 Western Land Claims

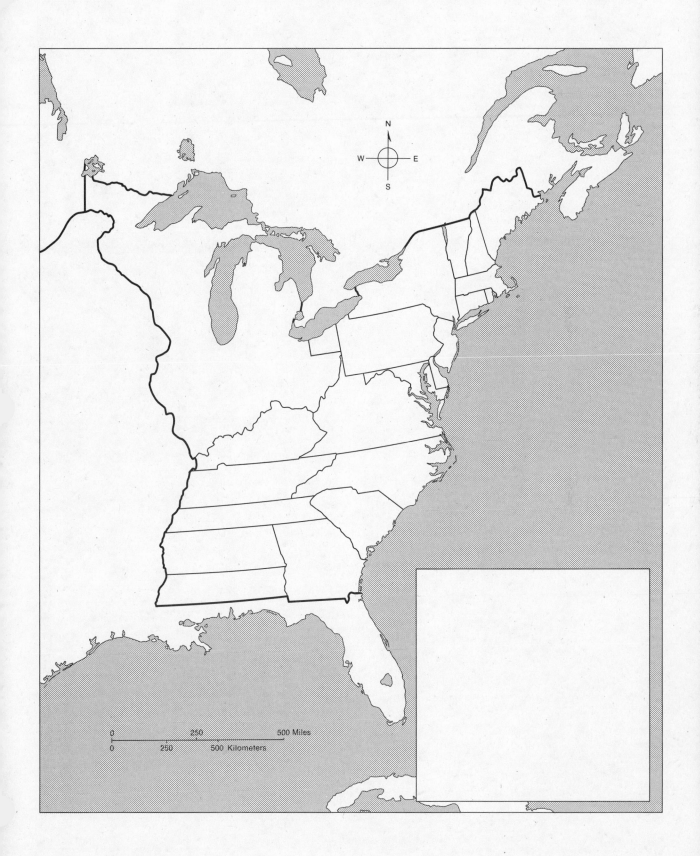

0   250   500 Miles
0   250   500 Kilometers

30 Exploring the Louisiana Purchase

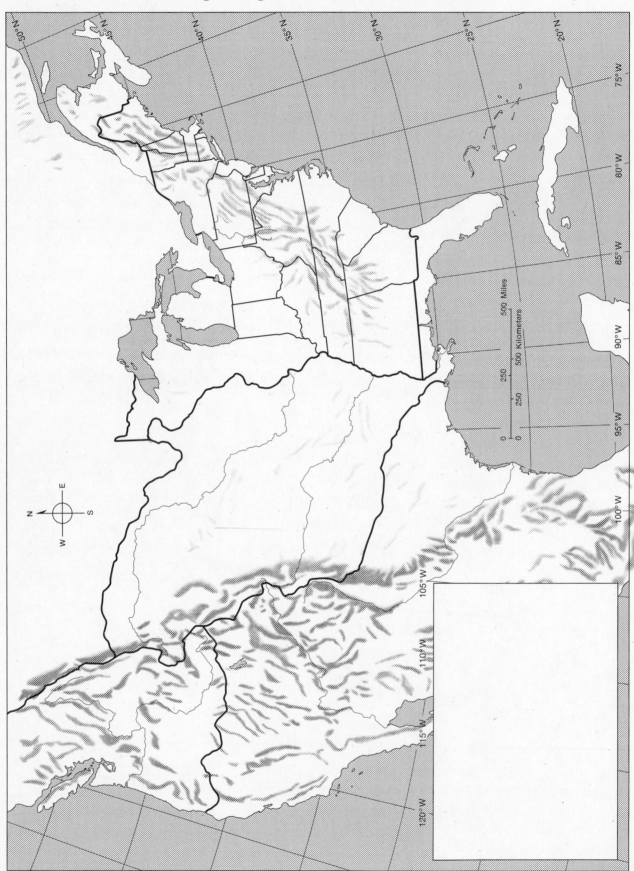

31 Land Acquired From Native Americans to 1810

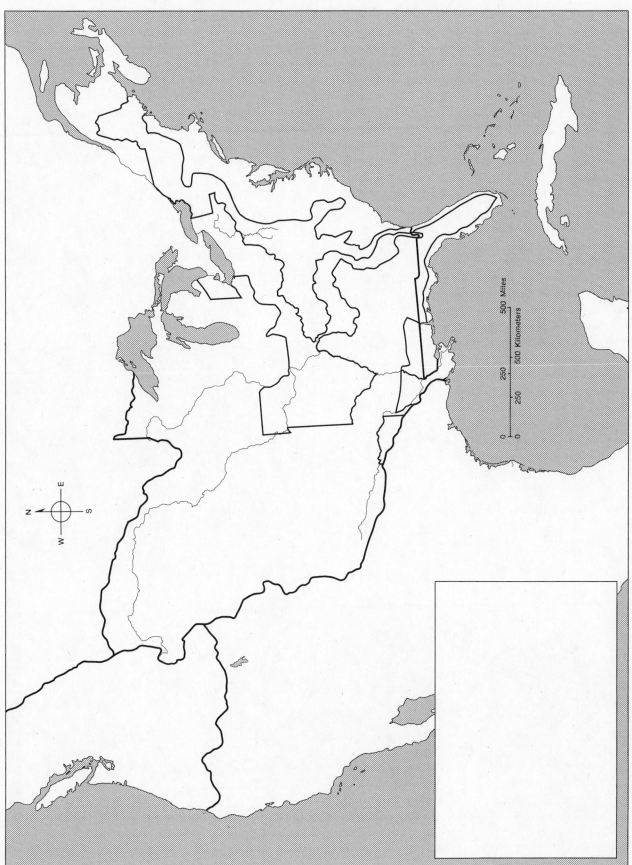

32 The War of 1812

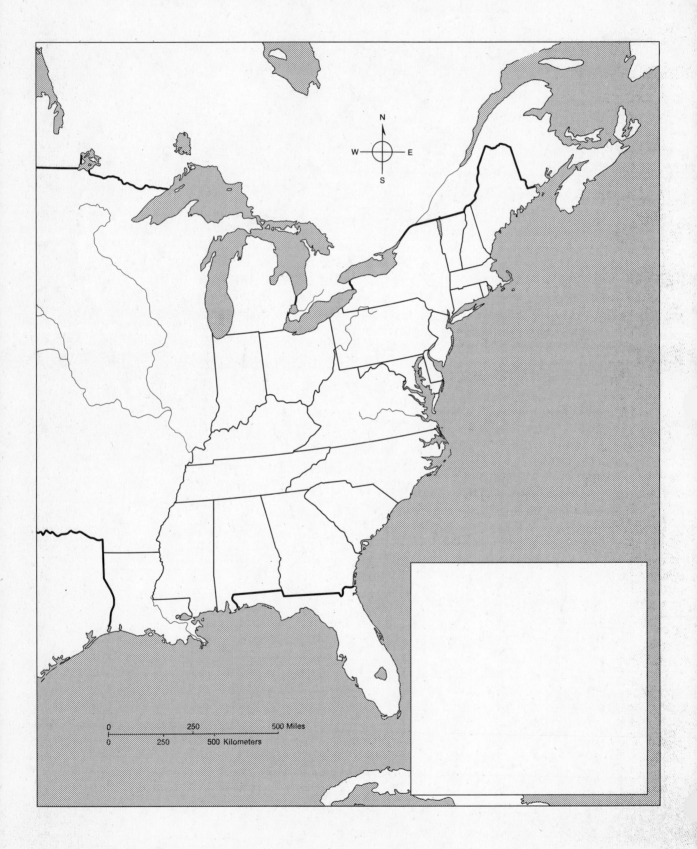

0   250   500 Miles

0   250   500 Kilometers

33 Transportation to the West

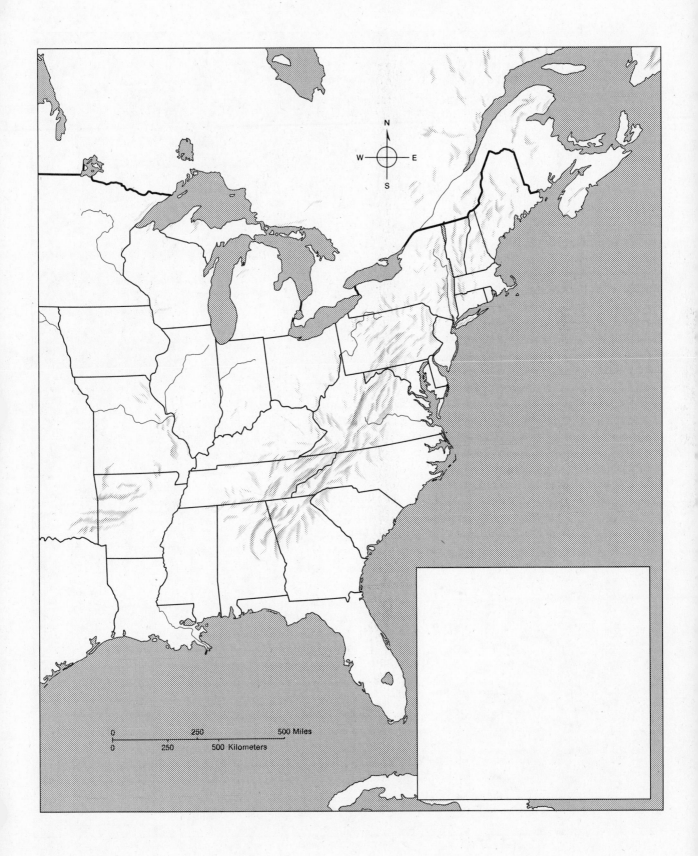

0   250   500 Miles

0   250   500 Kilometers

34 The United States in 1824

Name _____   Date _____

35 New Nations in Latin America

36 Election of 1828

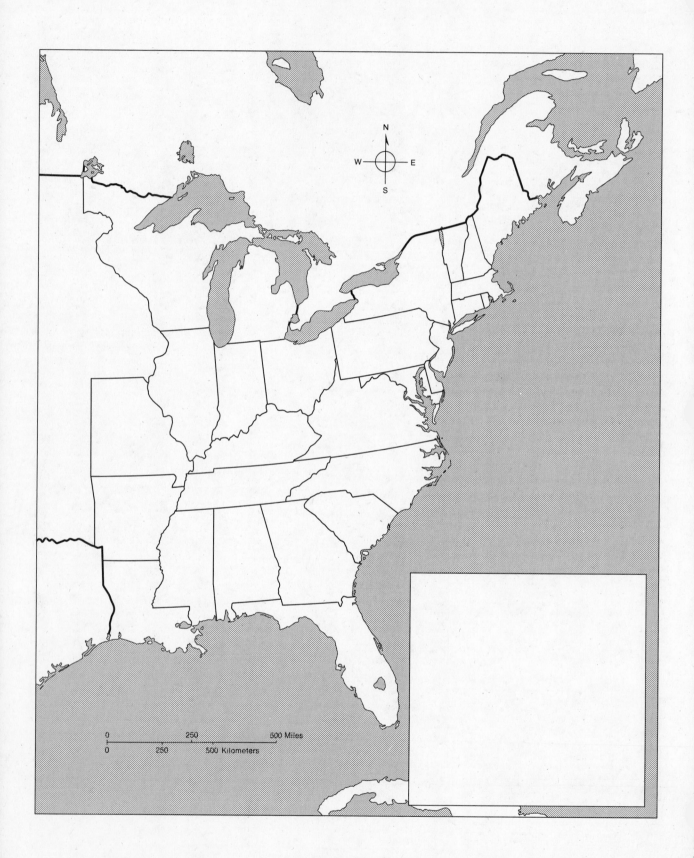

0   250   500 Miles

0   250   500 Kilometers

37 Indian Removal, 1830-1842

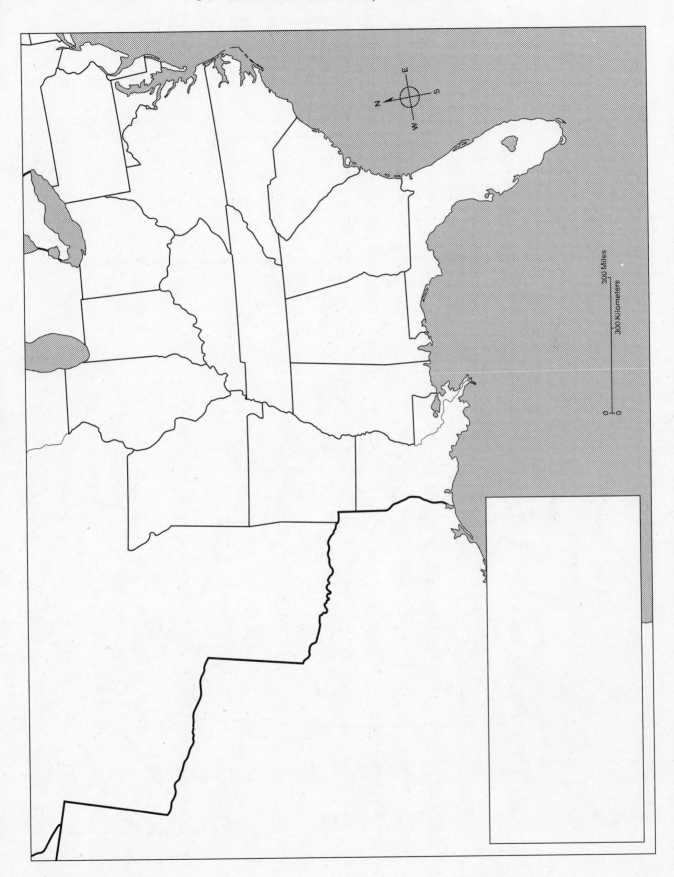

300 Miles

300 Kilometers

38 Oregon Country

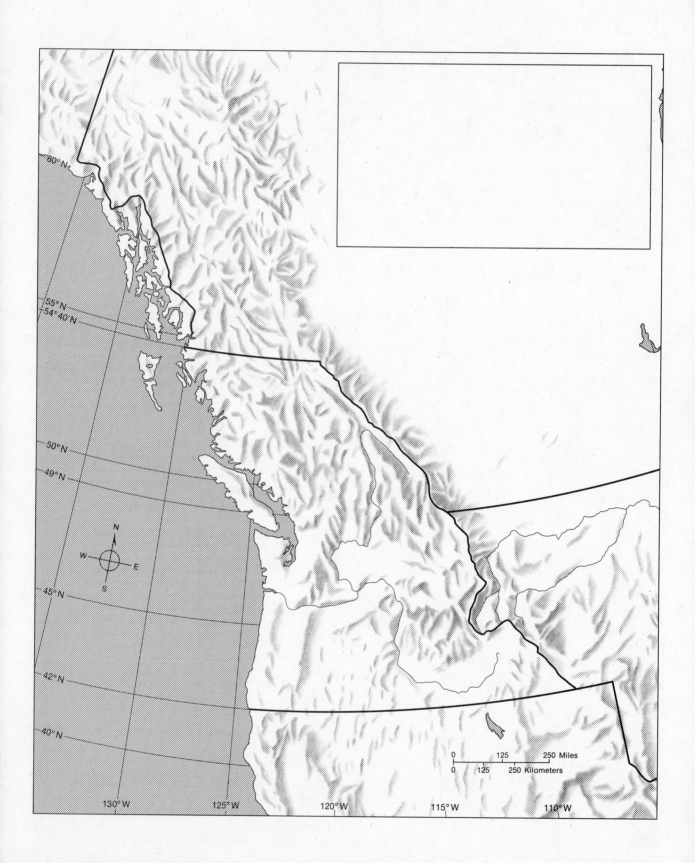

39 Independence for Texas

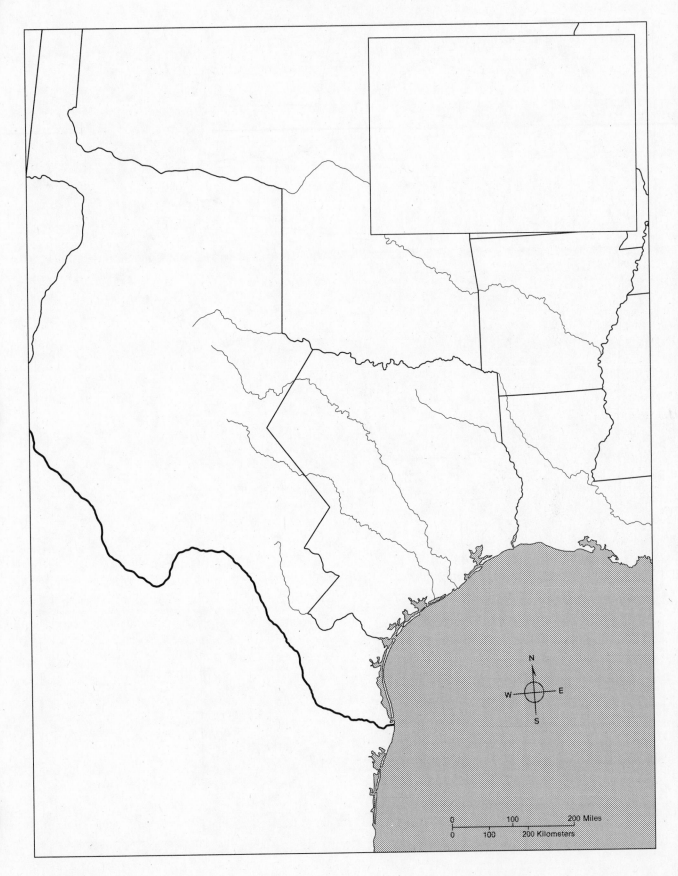

40 Trails to the West

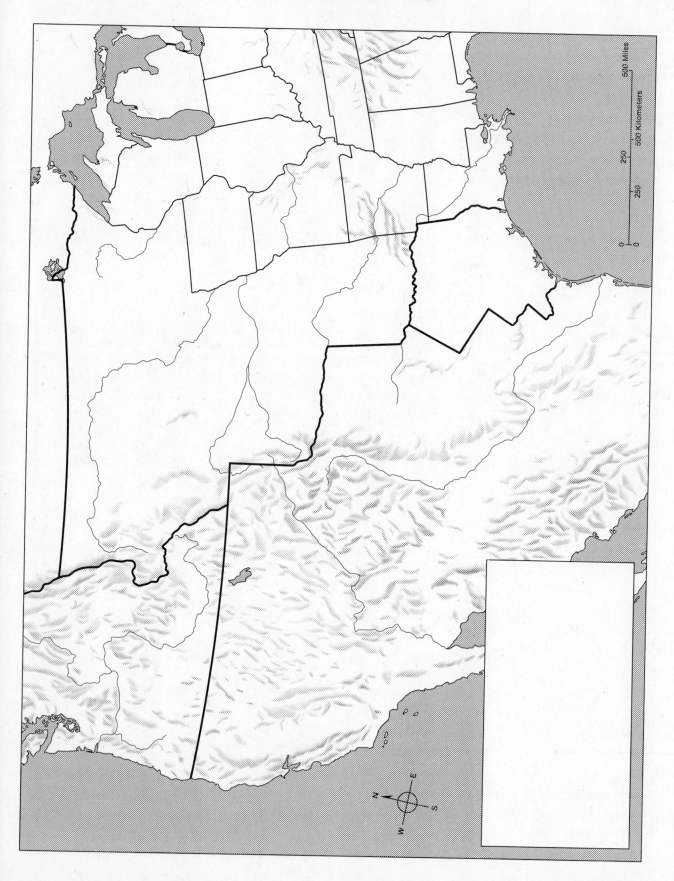

500 Miles

500 Kilometers

250

250

41 War with Mexico, 1846-1848

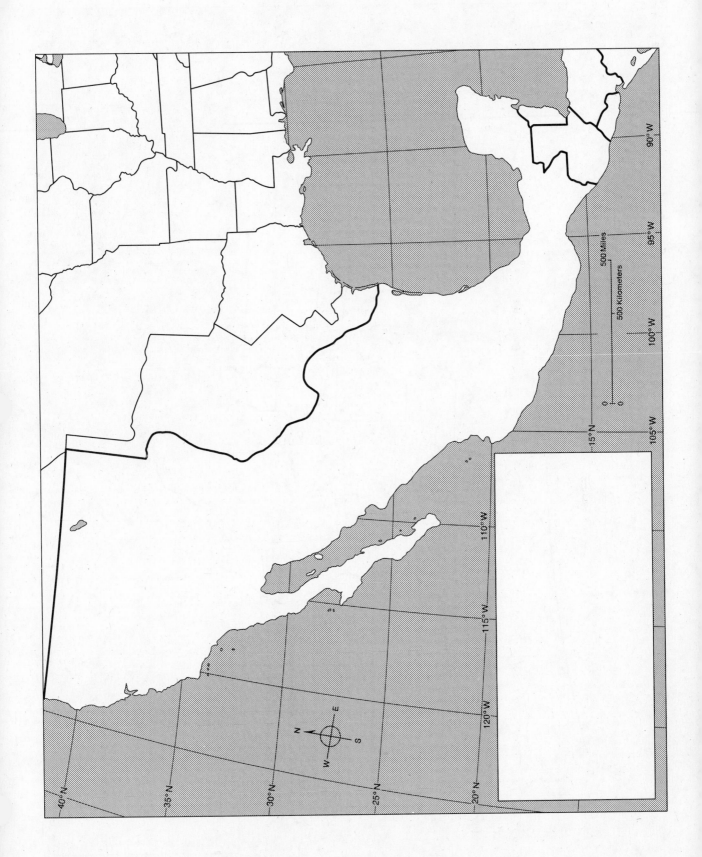

42 Growth of the United States to 1853

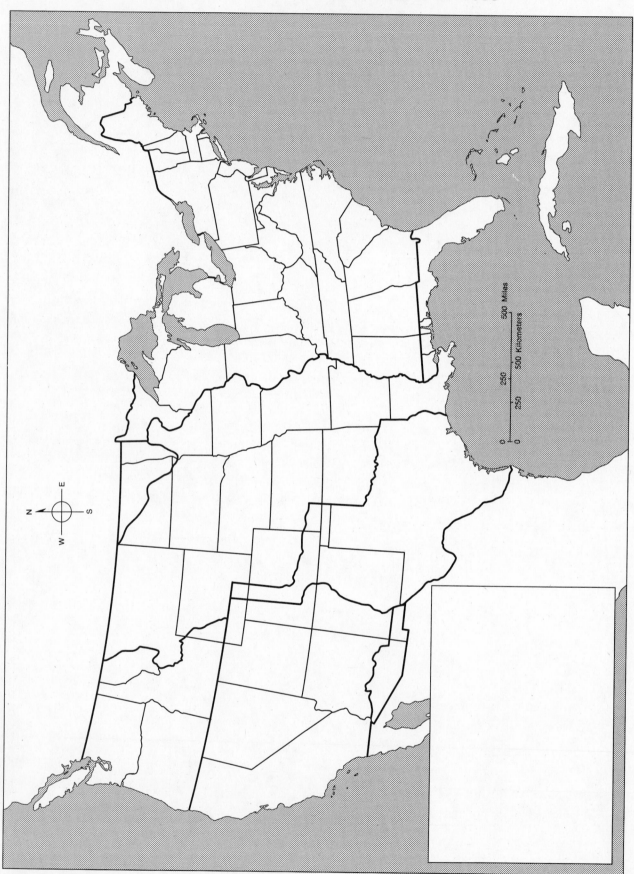

500 Miles
500 Kilometers
250
250
0
0

N E S W

43 The Northern States

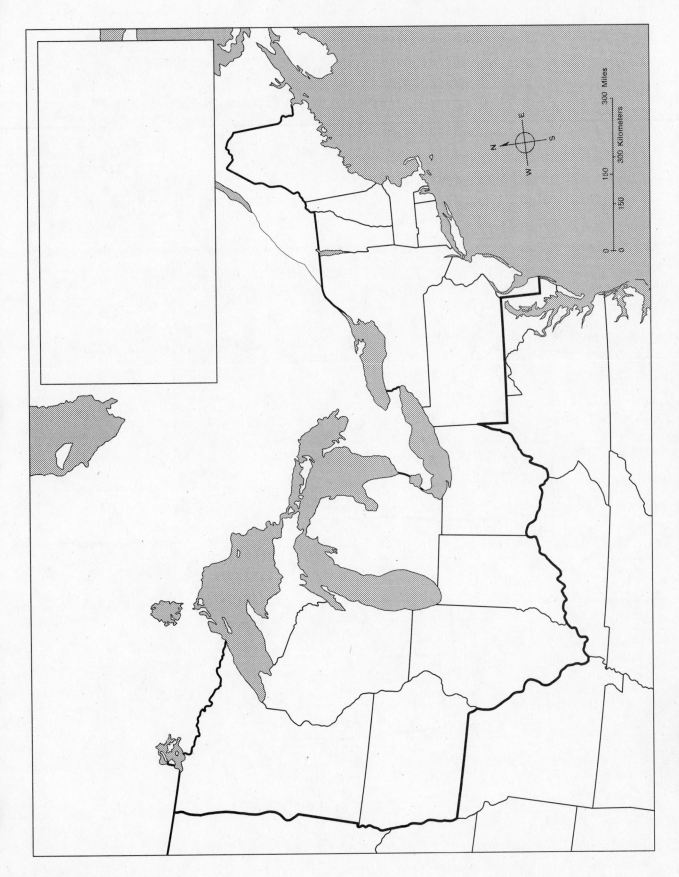

44 The Southern States

45 The Missouri Compromise, 1820

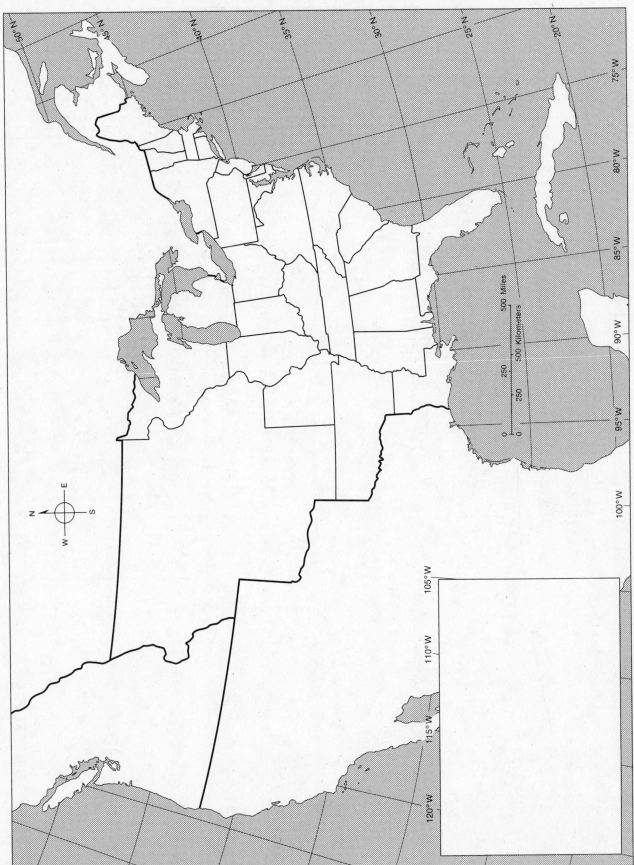

46 The Compromise of 1850

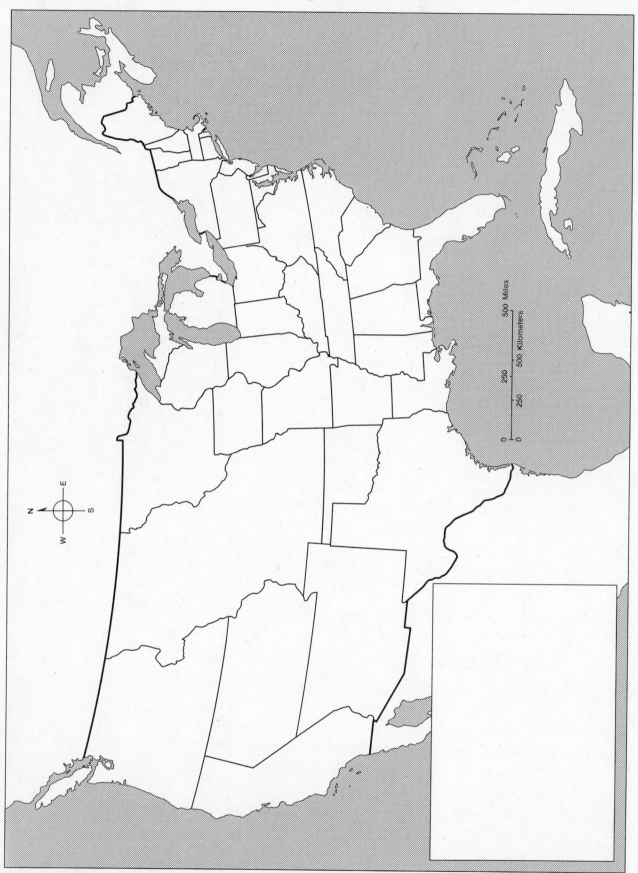

© Prentice-Hall, Inc.

47 Kansas-Nebraska Act, 1854

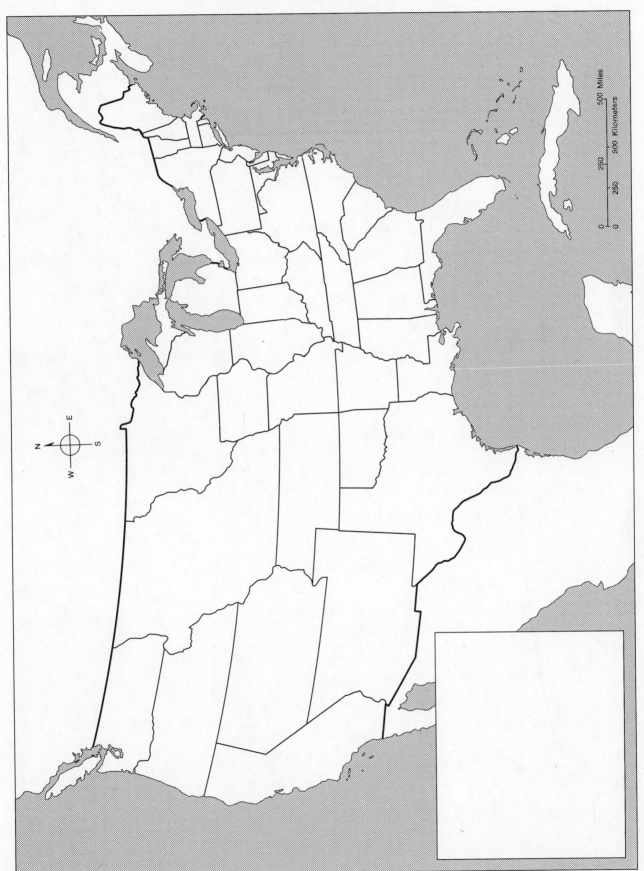

48 Election of 1860

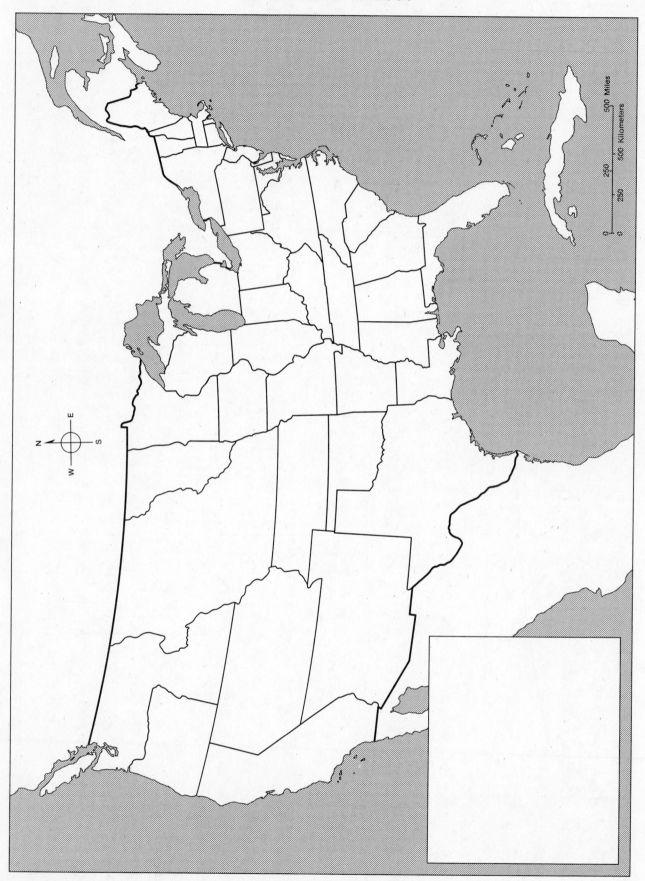

49 Choosing Sides

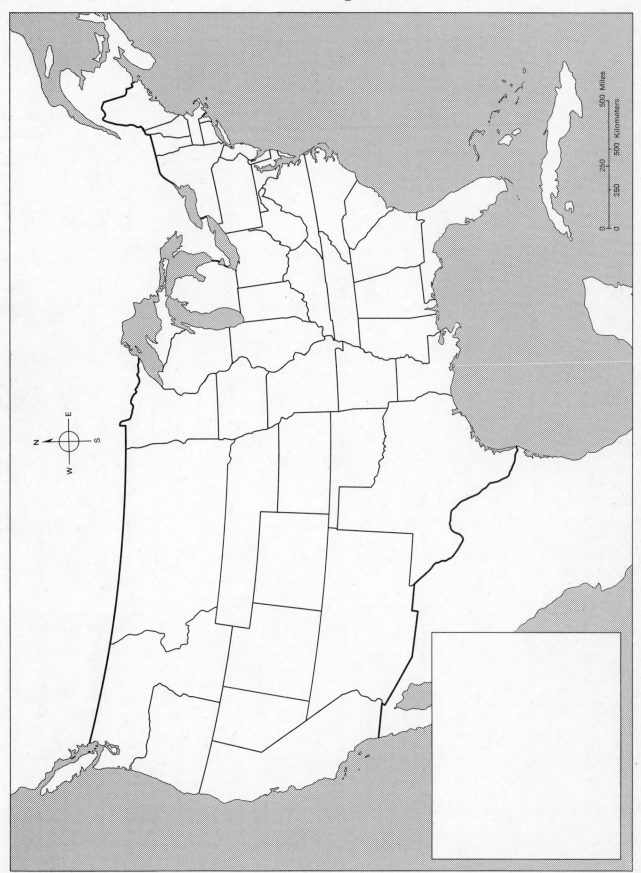

500 Miles
250
0
500 Kilometers
250
0

N
E
W
S

50 Major Battles of the Civil War

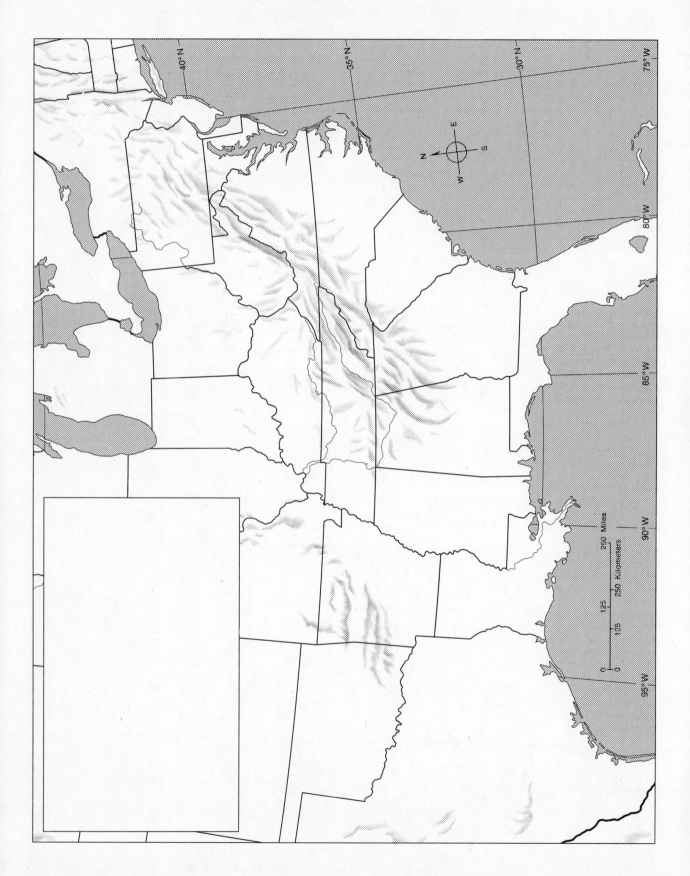

51 The Civil War in the East

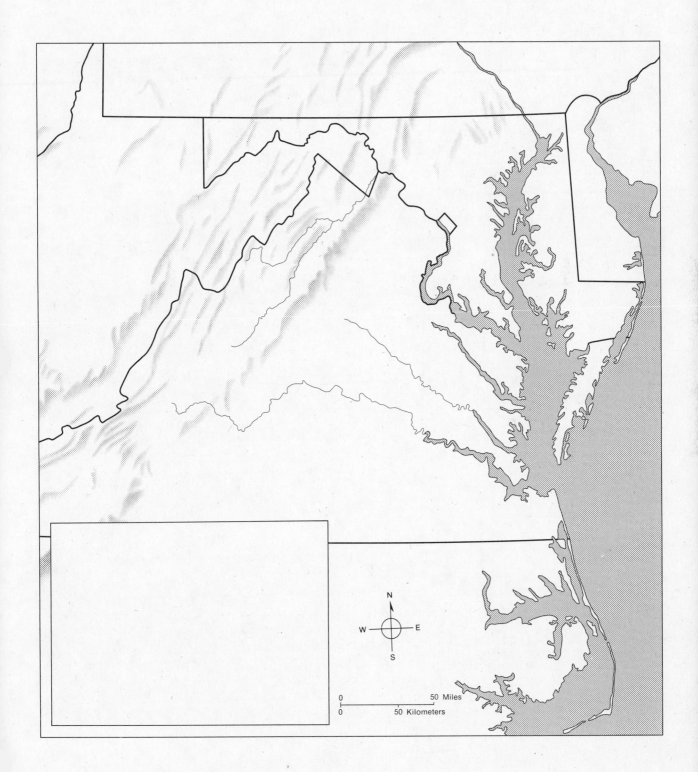

52 Union Advances

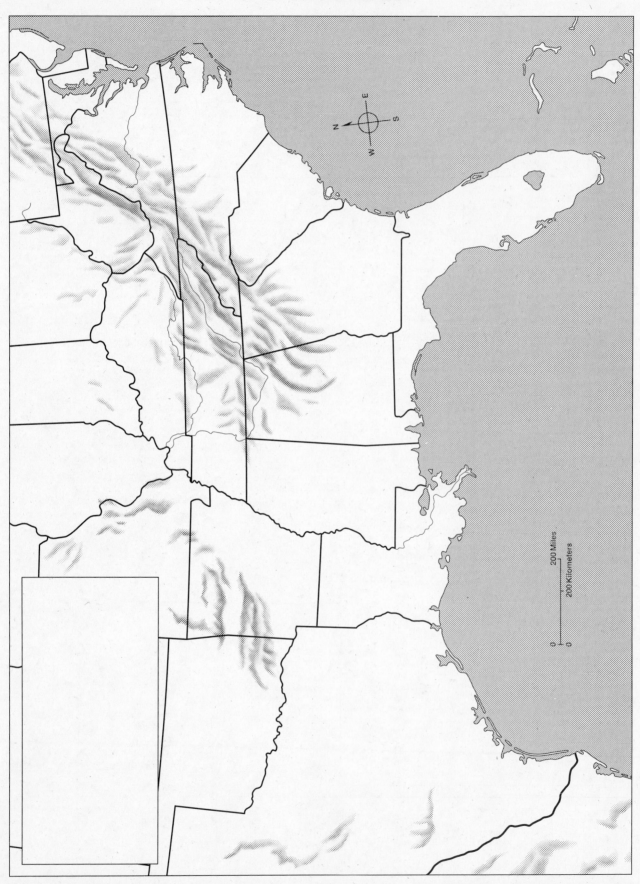

53 Reconstruction

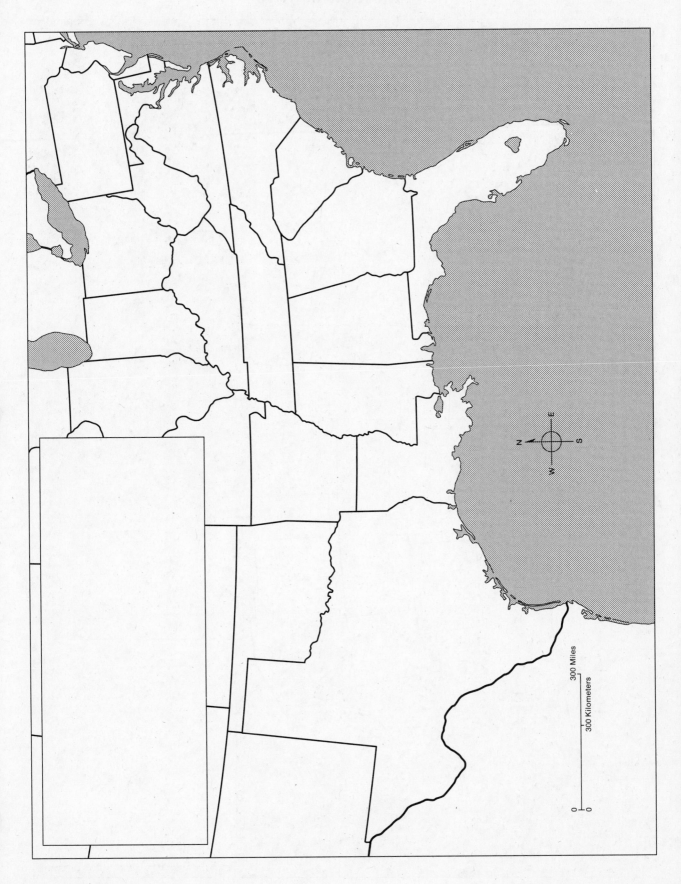

54 Election of 1876

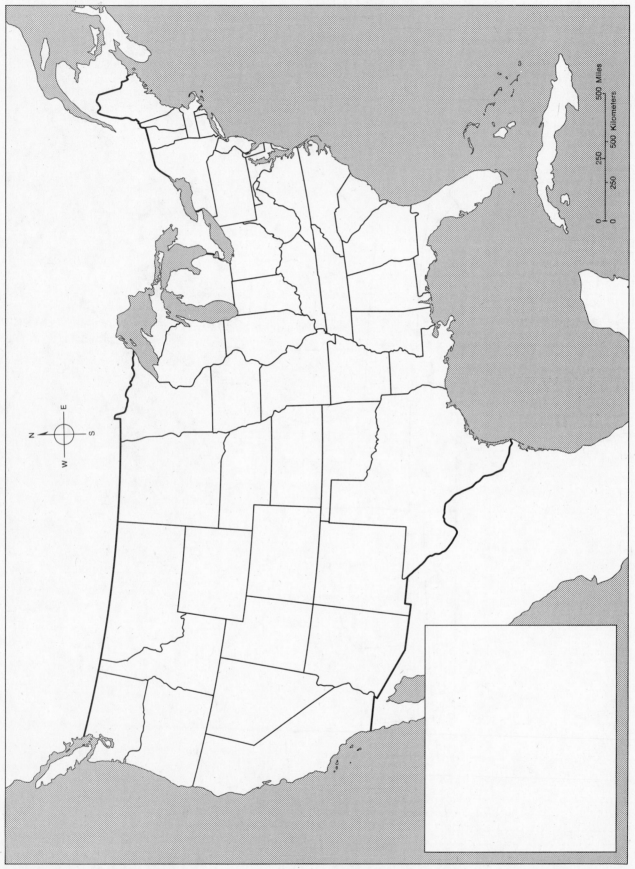

55 Indian Lands After 1850

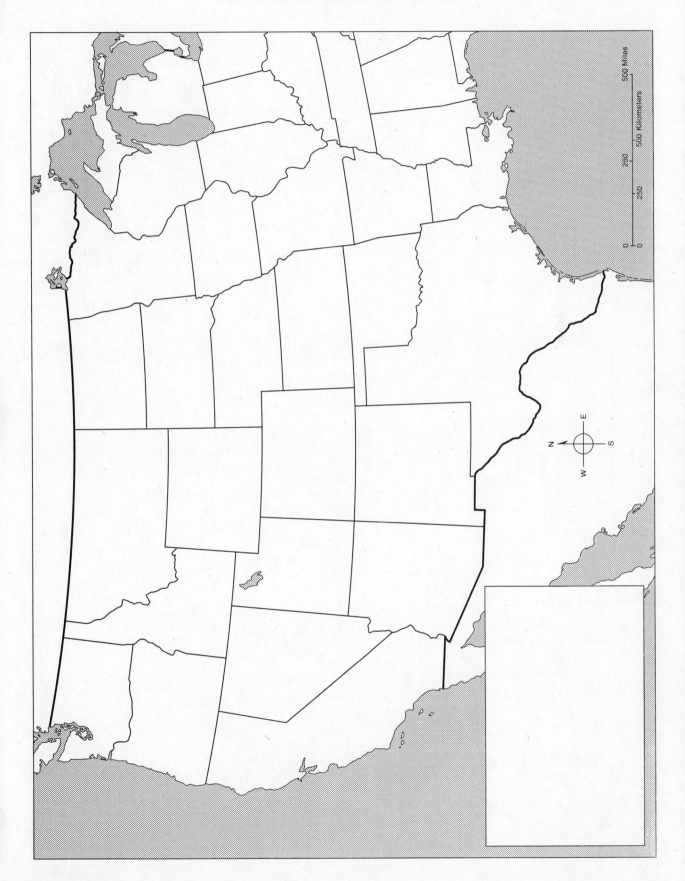

56 Opening the West

57 The Spanish-American War

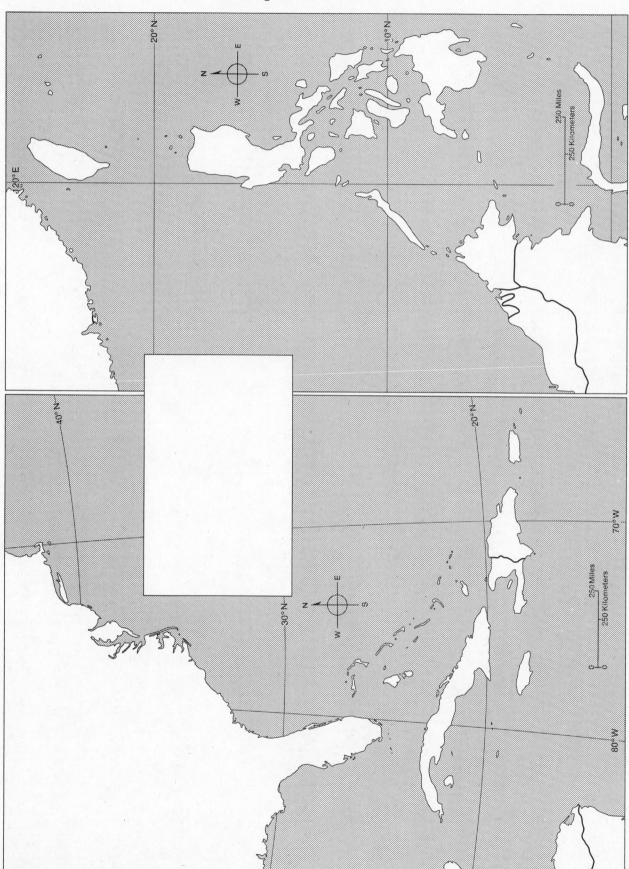

58 The United States in the Caribbean, 1898-1917

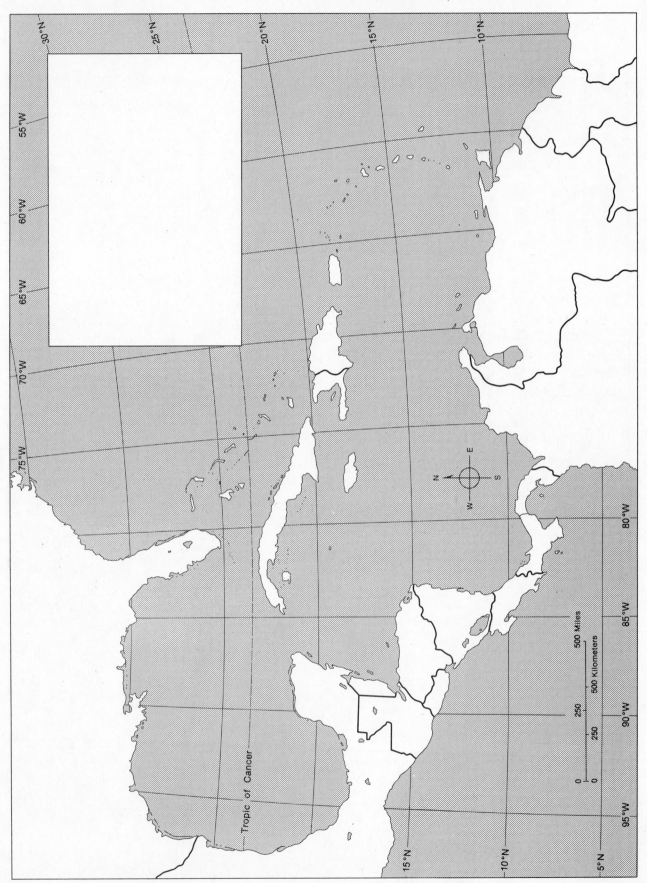

Tropic of Cancer

500 Miles
500 Kilometers
250
250
0
0

59 The Panama Canal

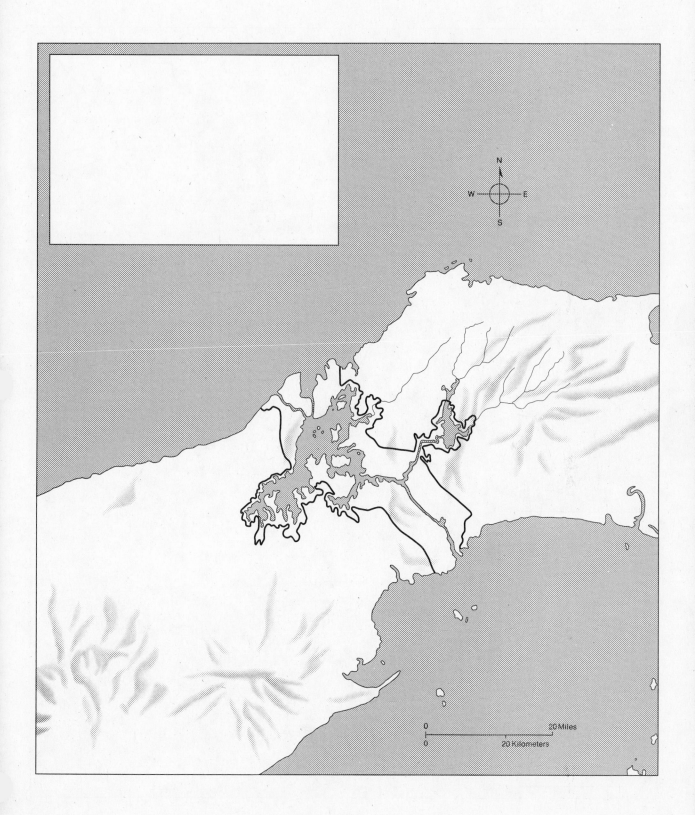

60 Europe in World War I

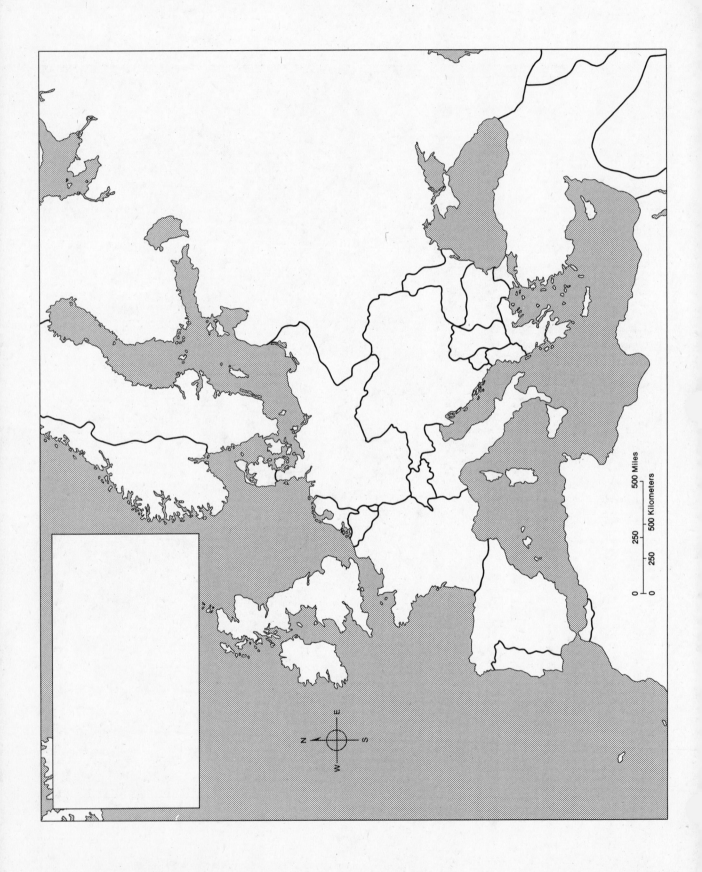

61 The Western Front, 1914-1918

0 — 25 — 50 Miles
0 — 25 — 50 Kilometers

62 Europe After World War I

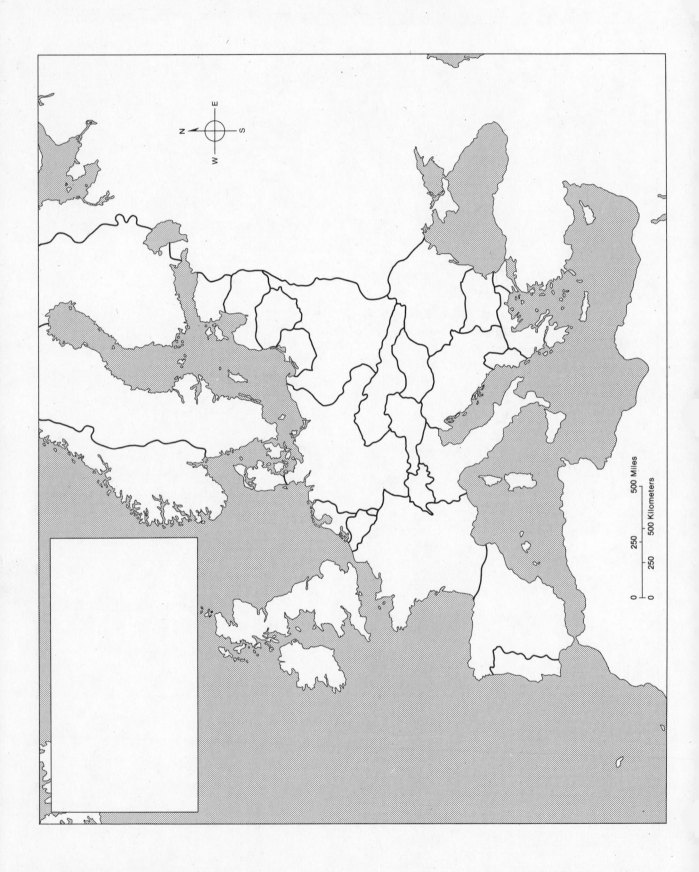

63 Tennessee Valley Authority

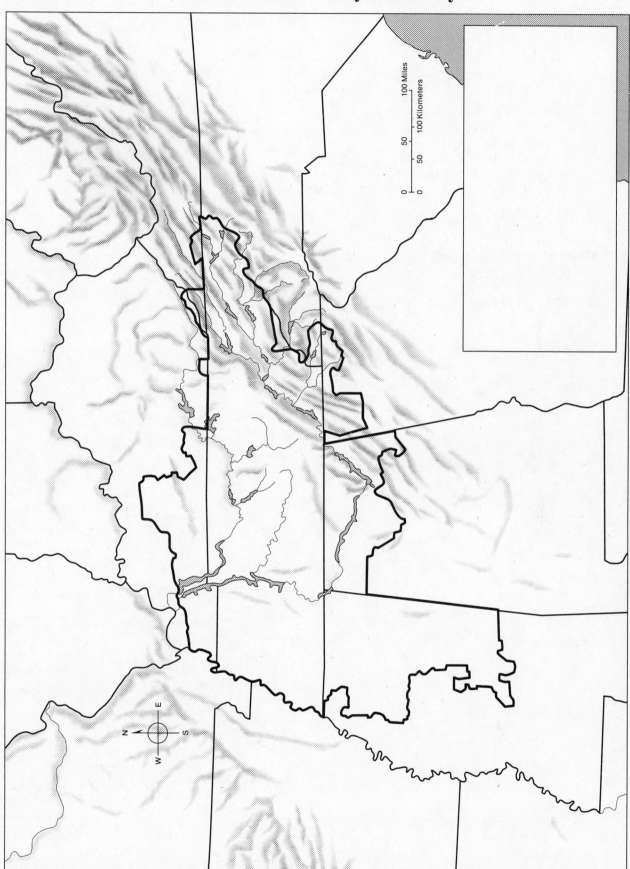

100 Miles

100 Kilometers

64 Aggression in Europe

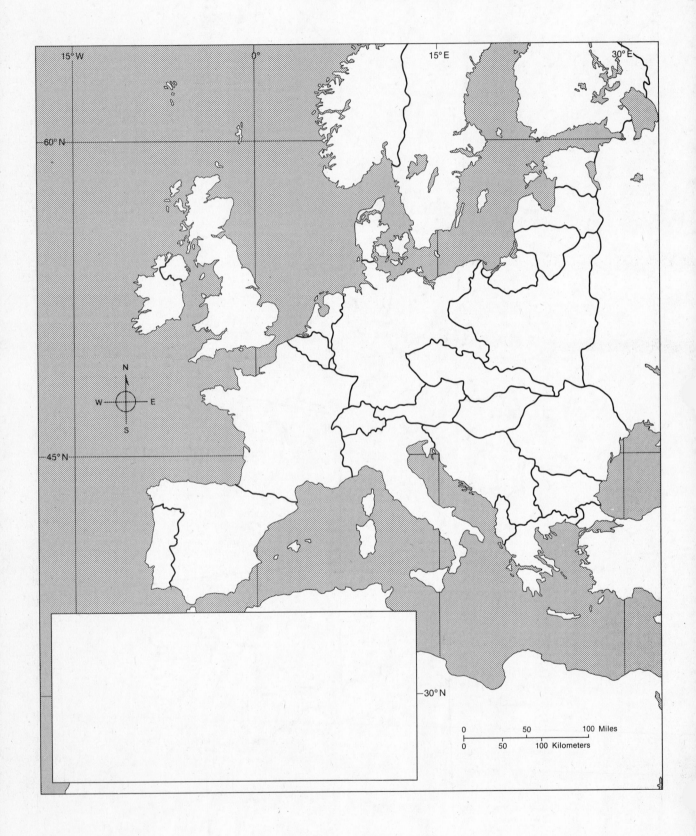

65 World War II in Europe and North Africa

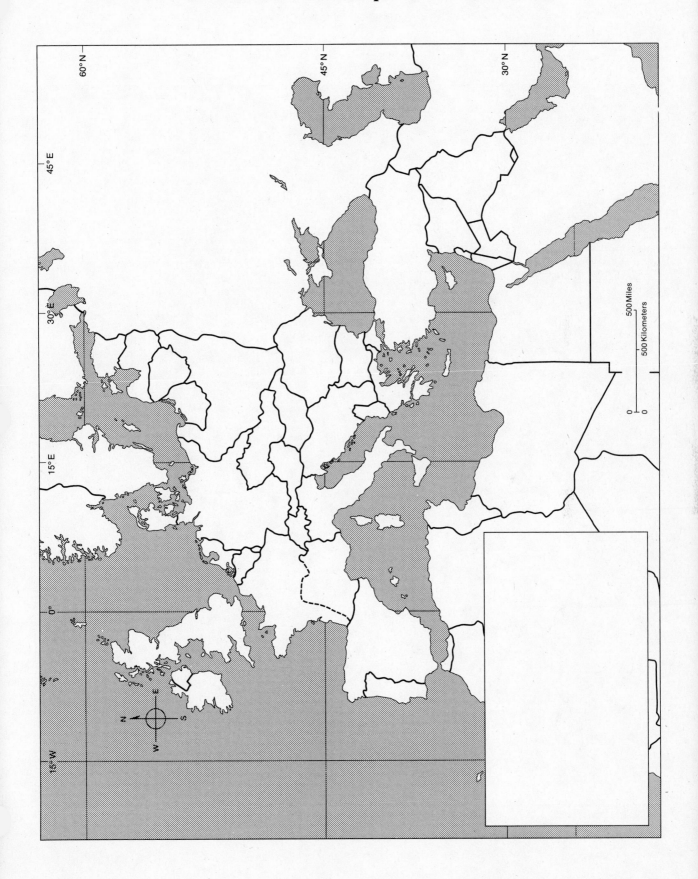

66 World War II in the Pacific

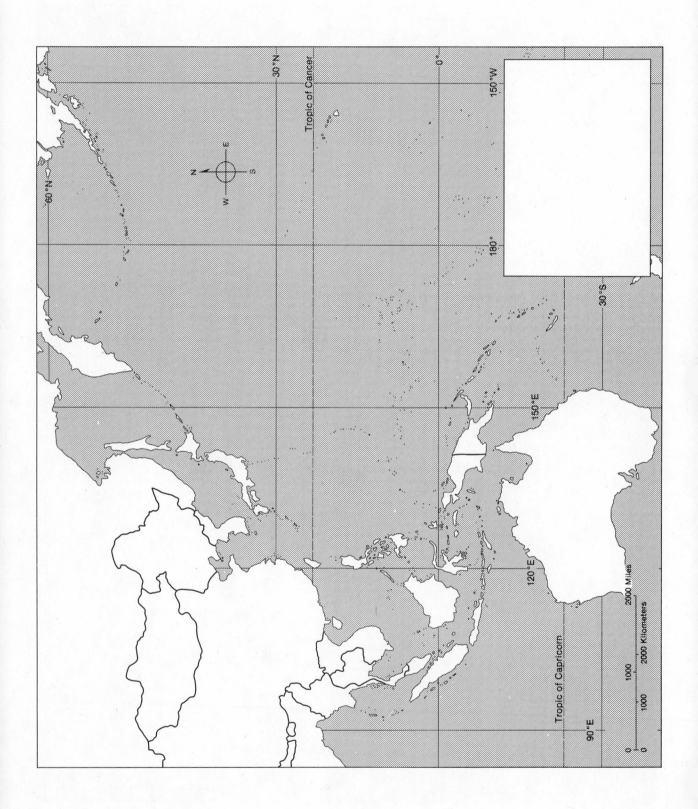

67 Germany Divided

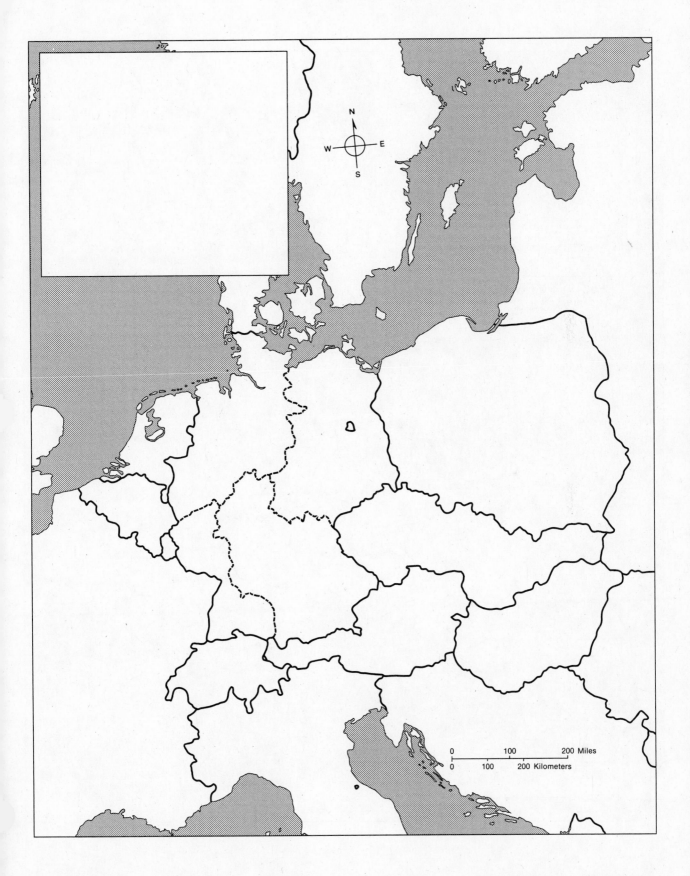

68 Europe After World War II

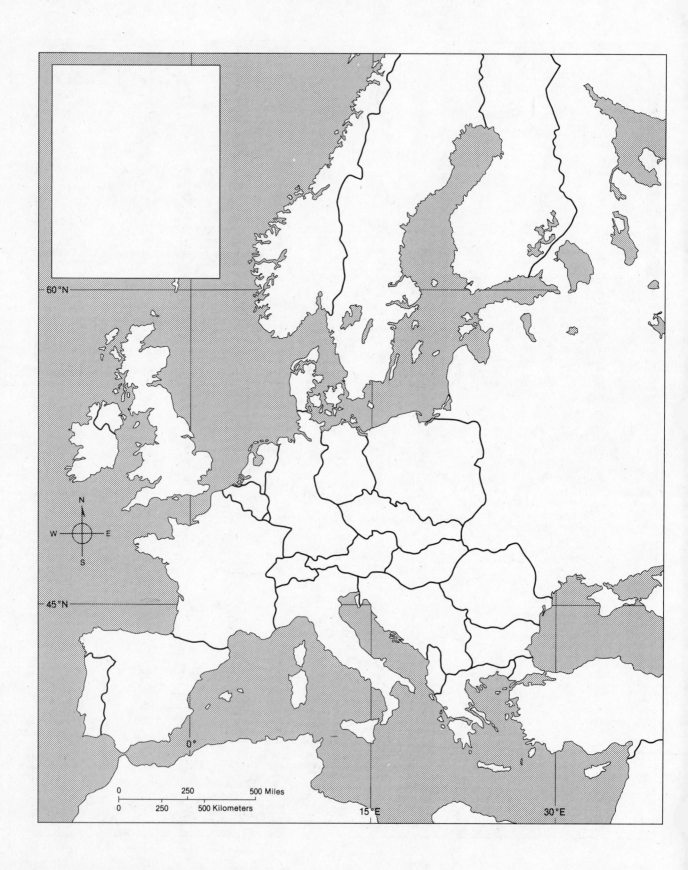

69 The Korean War

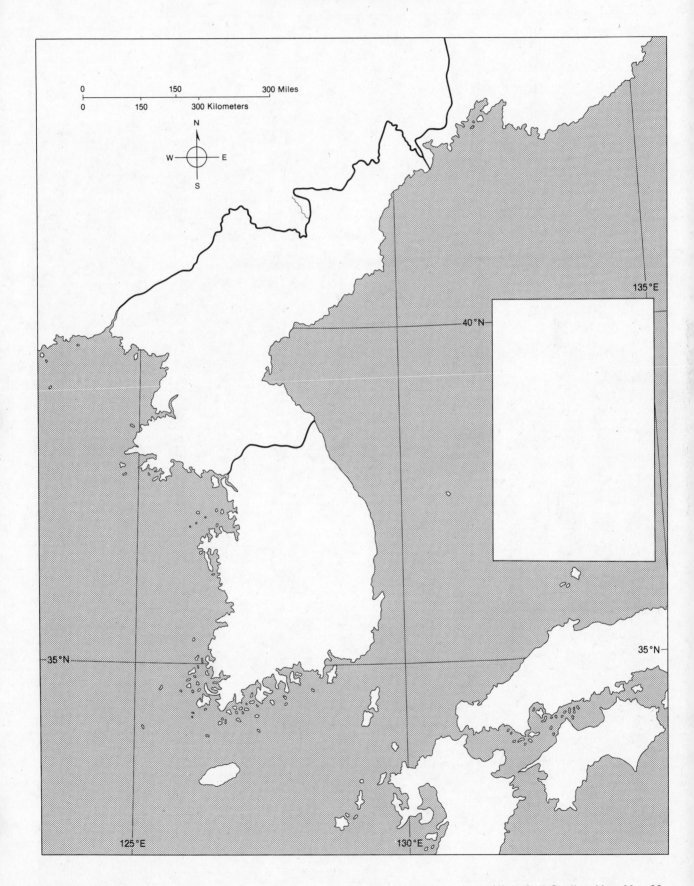

70 War in Southeast Asia

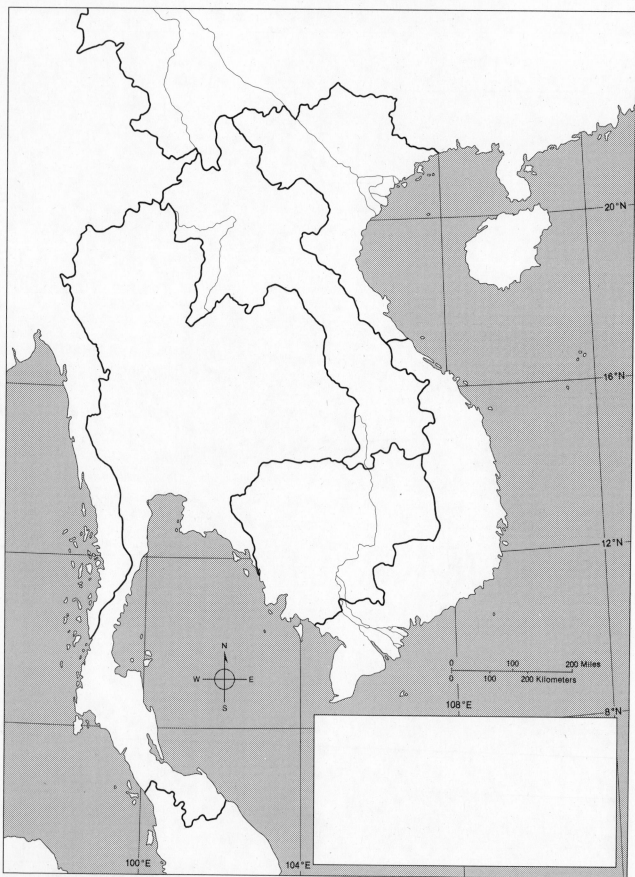

71 The World

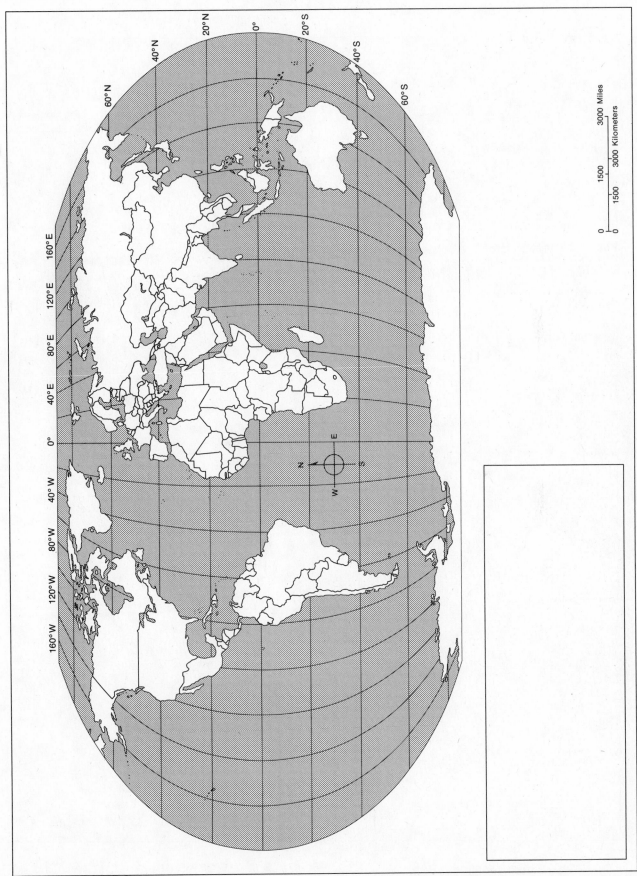

60°N

40°N

20°N

0°

20°S

40°S

60°S

160°E 120°E 80°E 40°E 0° 40°W 80°W 120°W 160°W

N E S W

3000 Miles
1500
0

3000 Kilometers
1500
0

72 Western Hemisphere

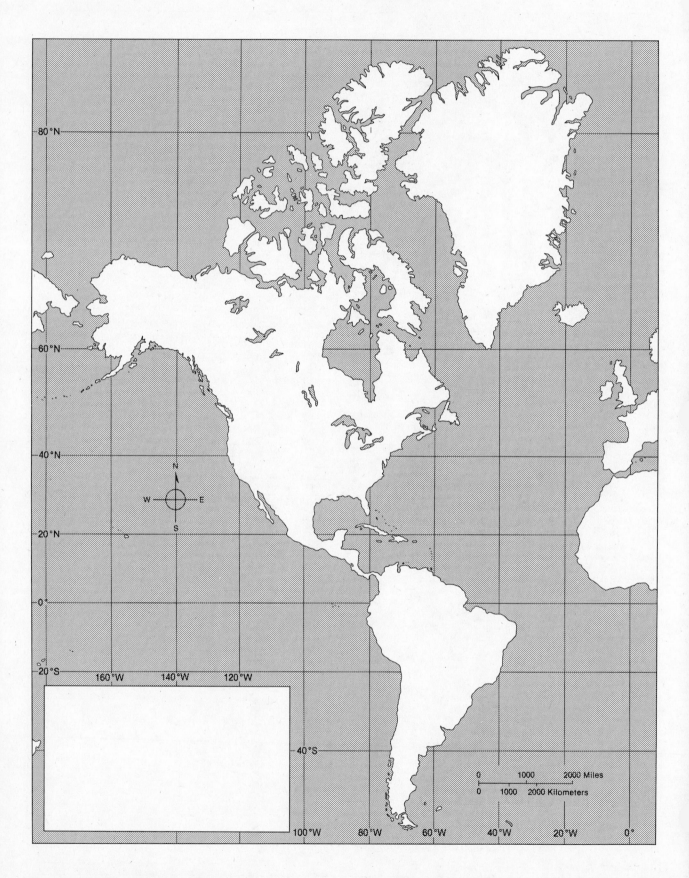

80°N

60°N

40°N

N
W   E
S

20°N

0°

20°S

160°W   140°W   120°W

40°S

0   1000   2000 Miles
0   1000   2000 Kilometers

100°W   80°W   60°W   40°W   20°W   0°

73 Eastern Hemisphere

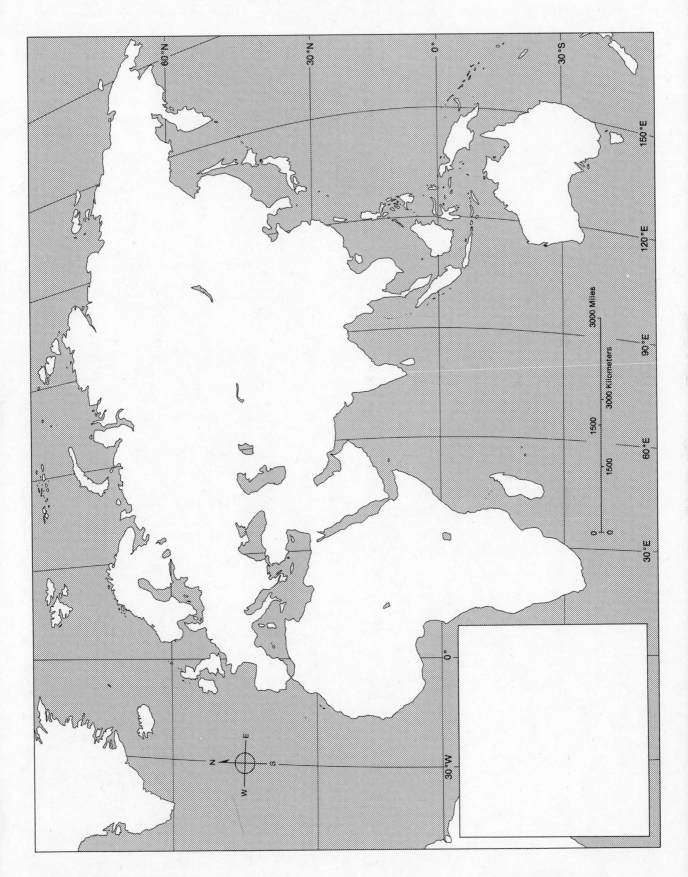

74 Africa

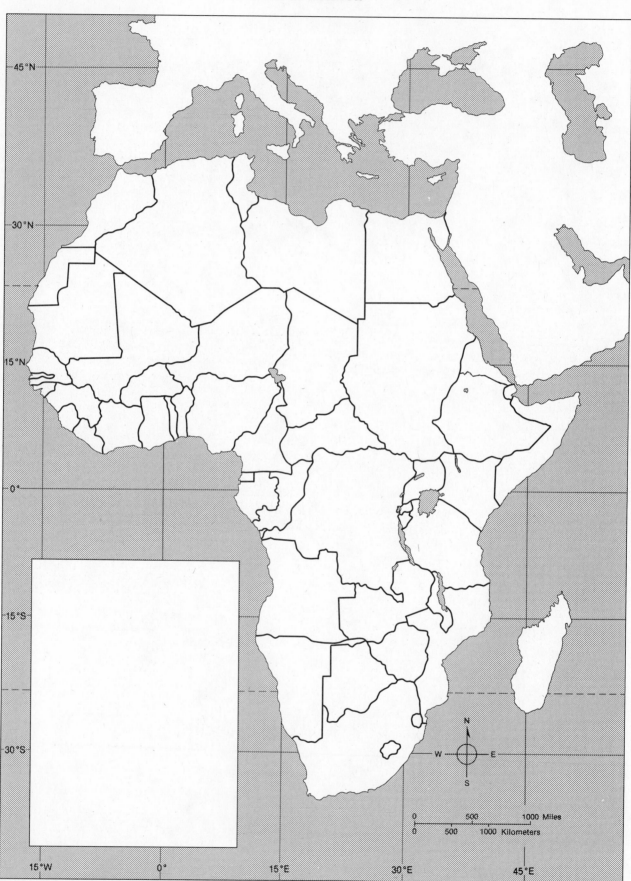

© Prentice-Hall, Inc.

75 Asia

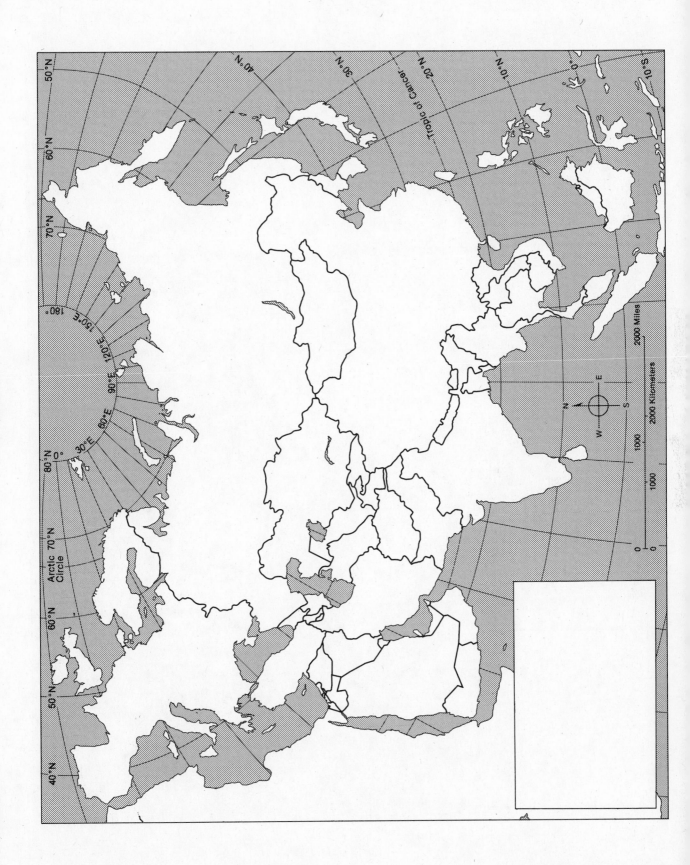

76 East Asia

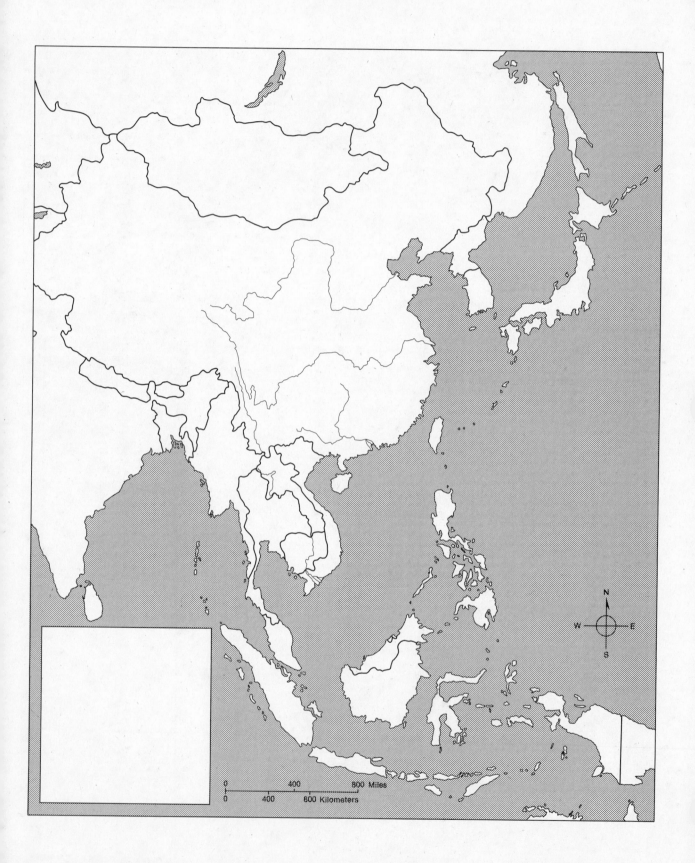

0   400   800 Miles
0   400   600 Kilometers

77 Europe

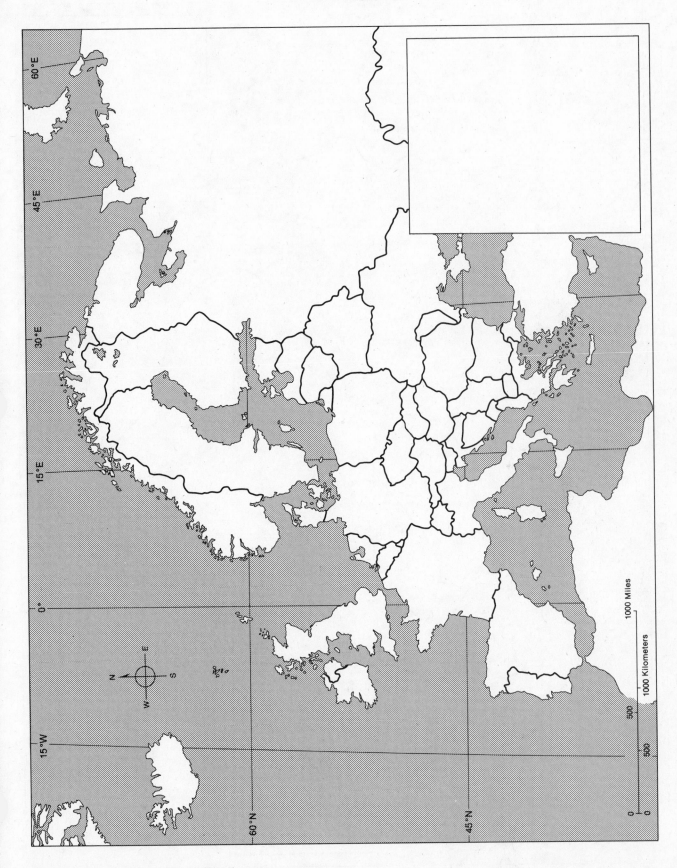

60°E

45°E

30°E

15°E

0°

15°W

60°N

45°N

1000 Miles

1000 Kilometers

500

500

0

0

78 The Middle East

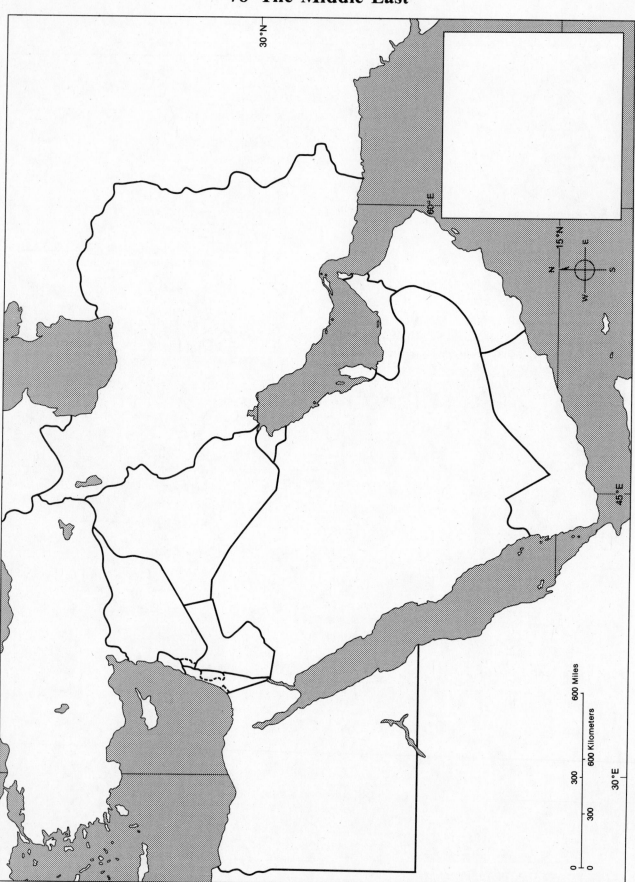

30°N

60°E

15°N

N
W · E
S

45°E

600 Miles

600 Kilometers

300

300

30°E

0
0

© Prentice-Hall, Inc.

79 North America

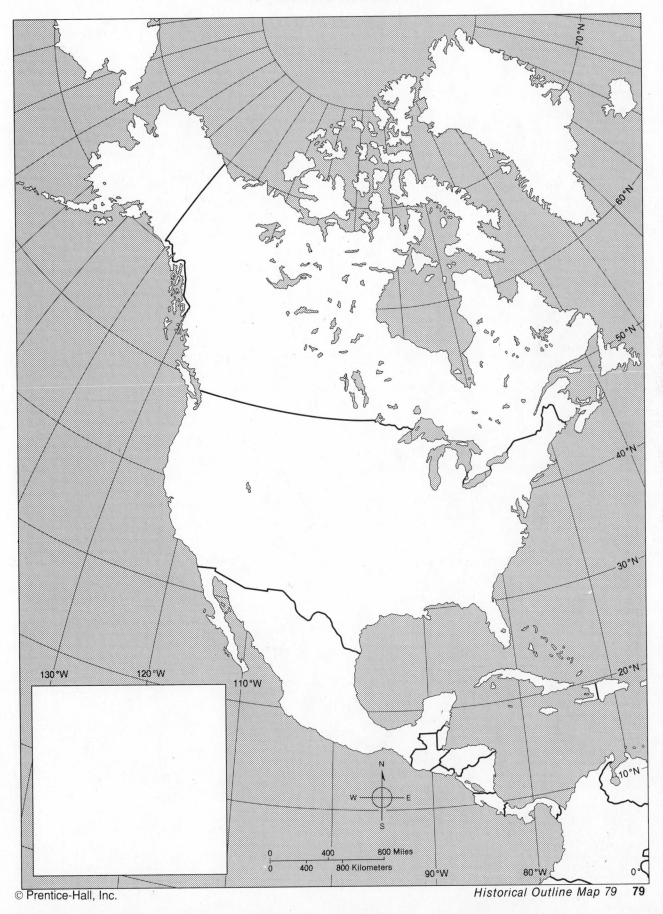

80 South America

81 Central America and the Caribbean

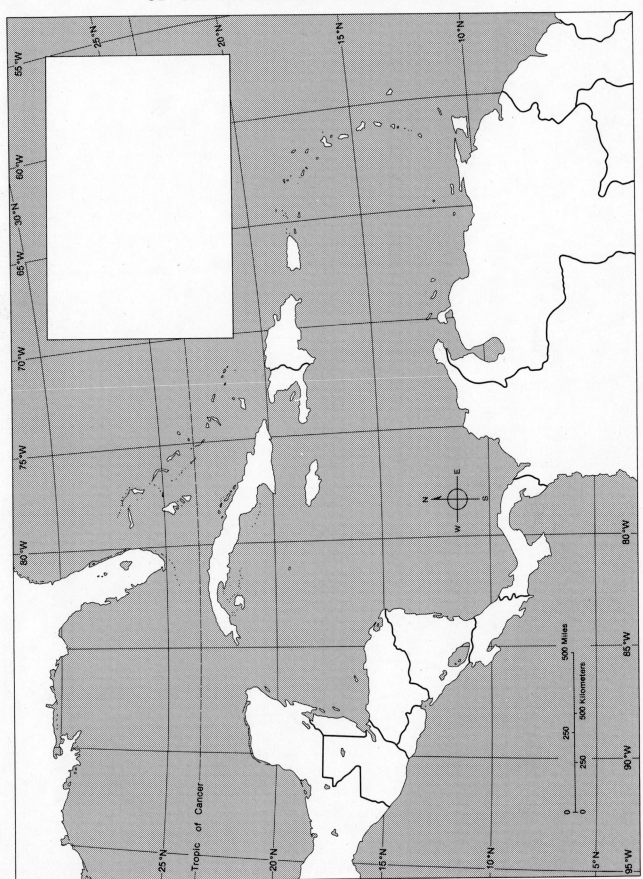

82 Political United States

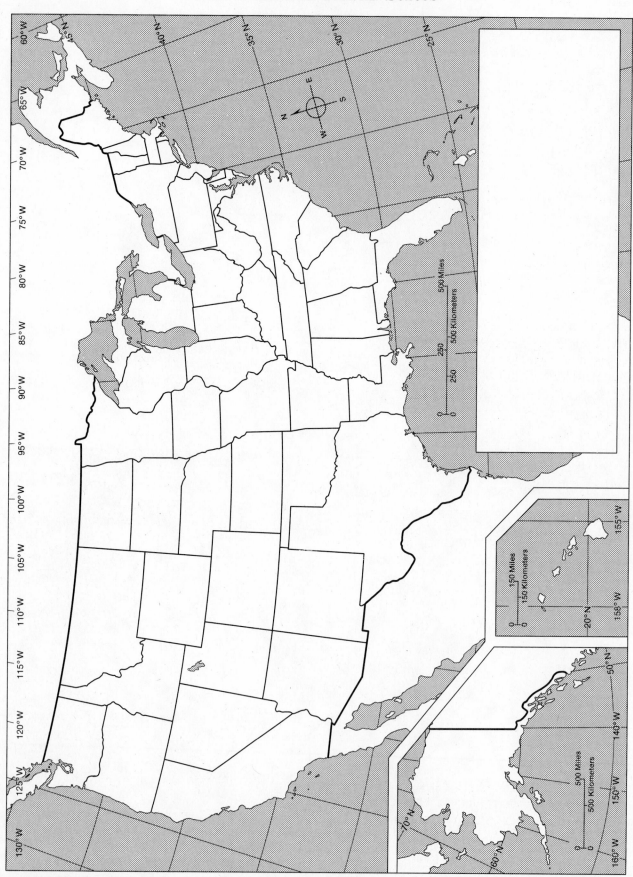

© Prentice-Hall, Inc.

83 Physical United States

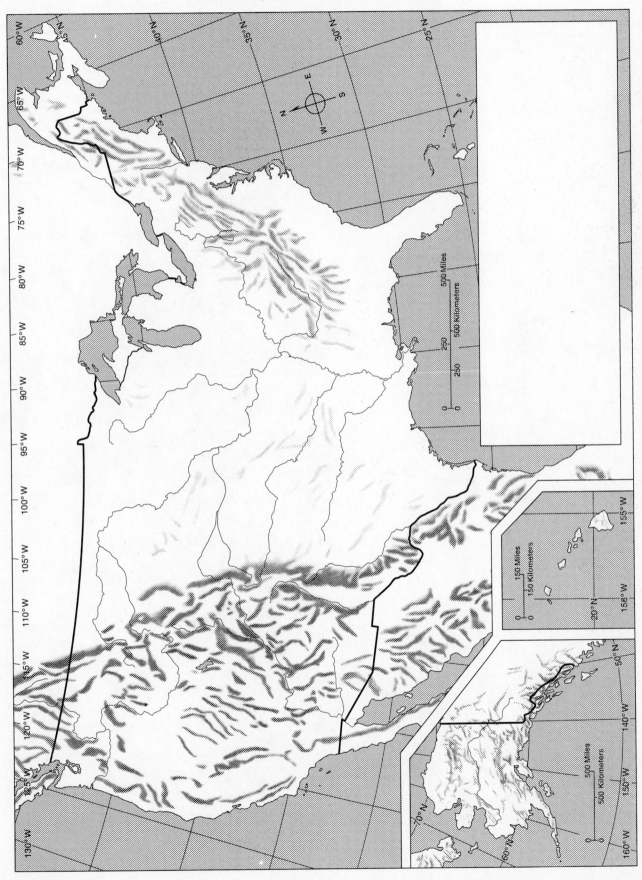

84 Eastern United States

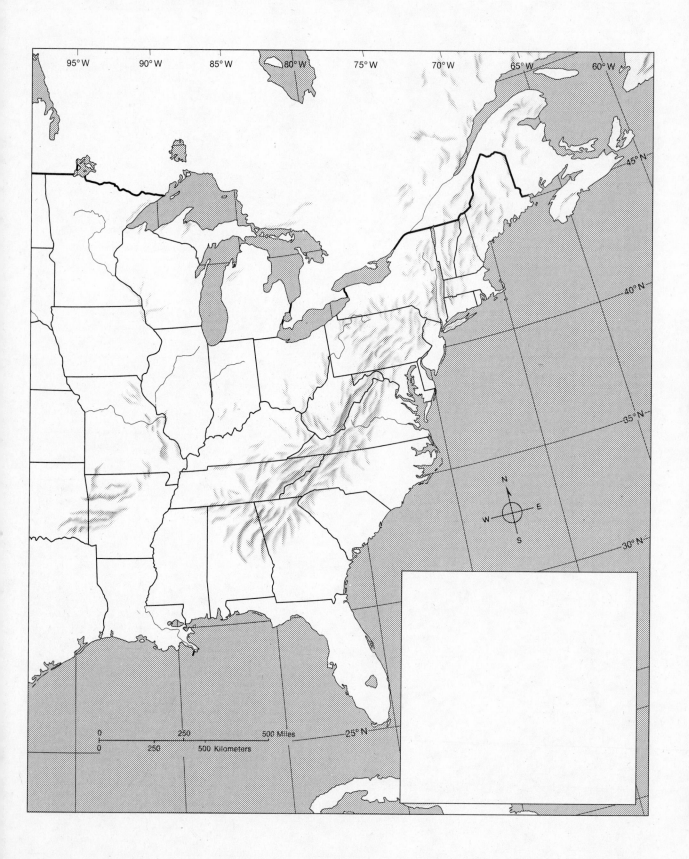

© Prentice-Hall, Inc.

85 Western United States

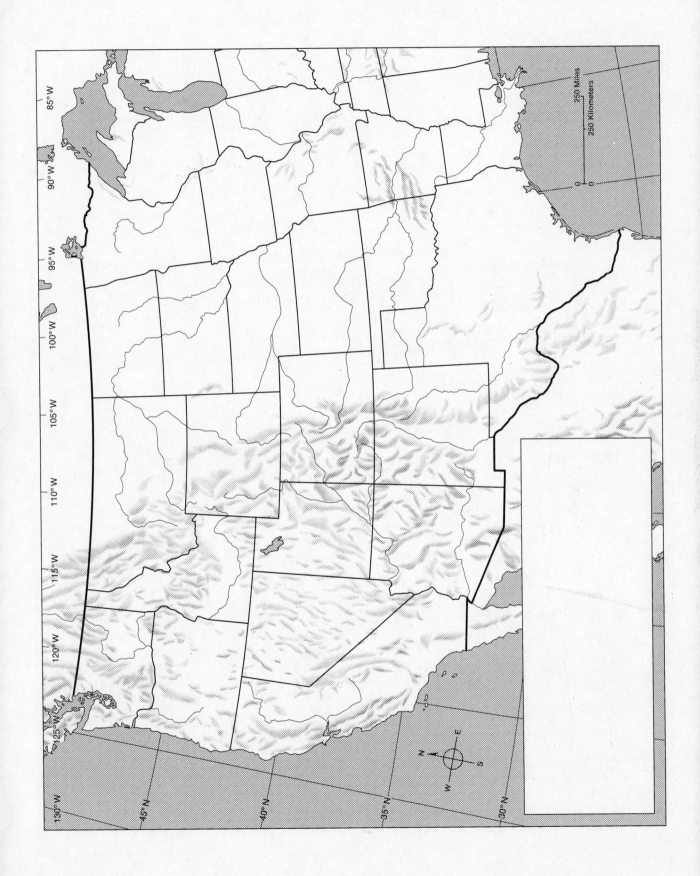

86 New England States

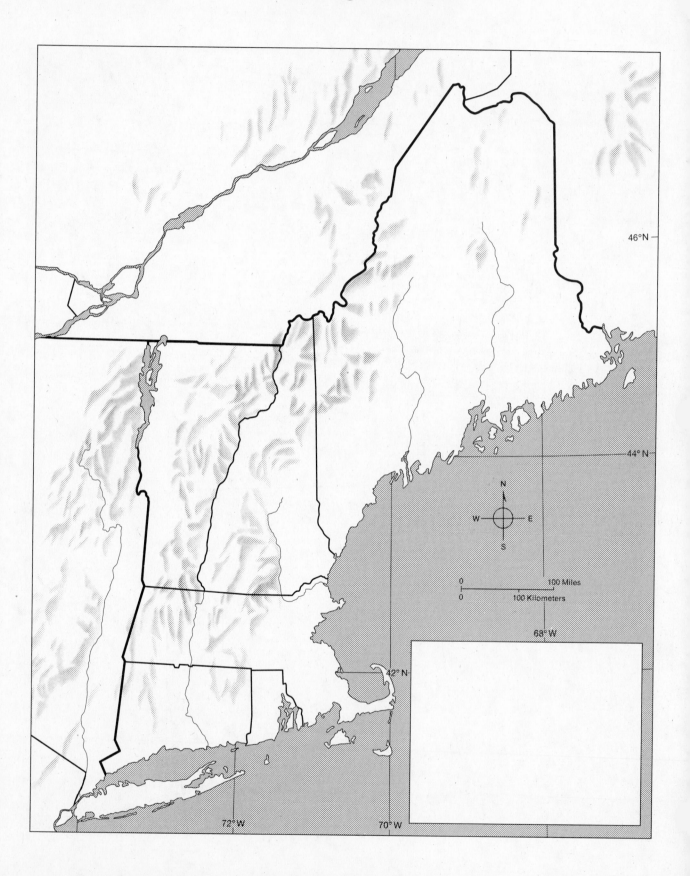

87 Middle Atlantic States

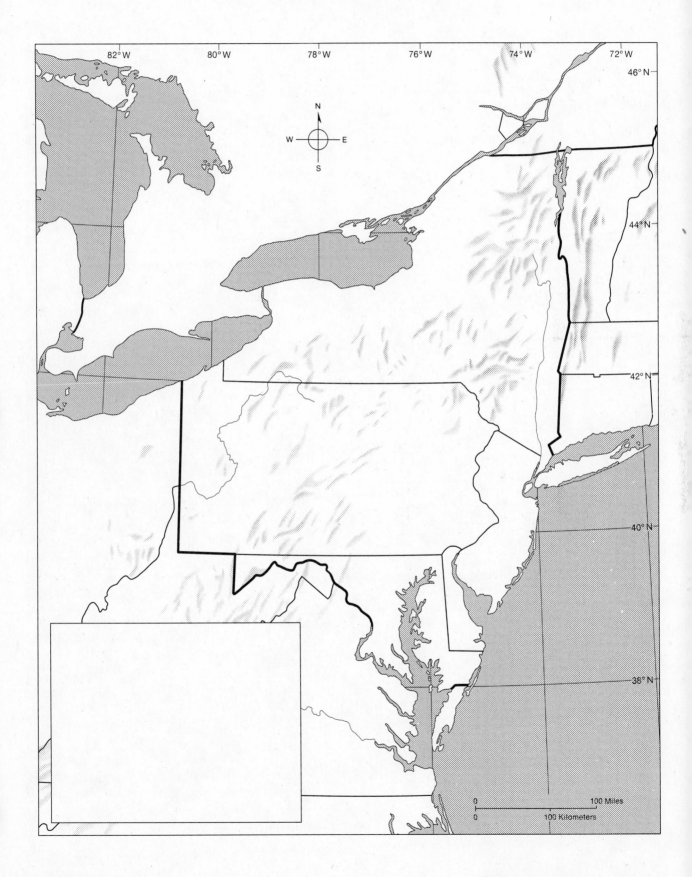

88 Southeastern States

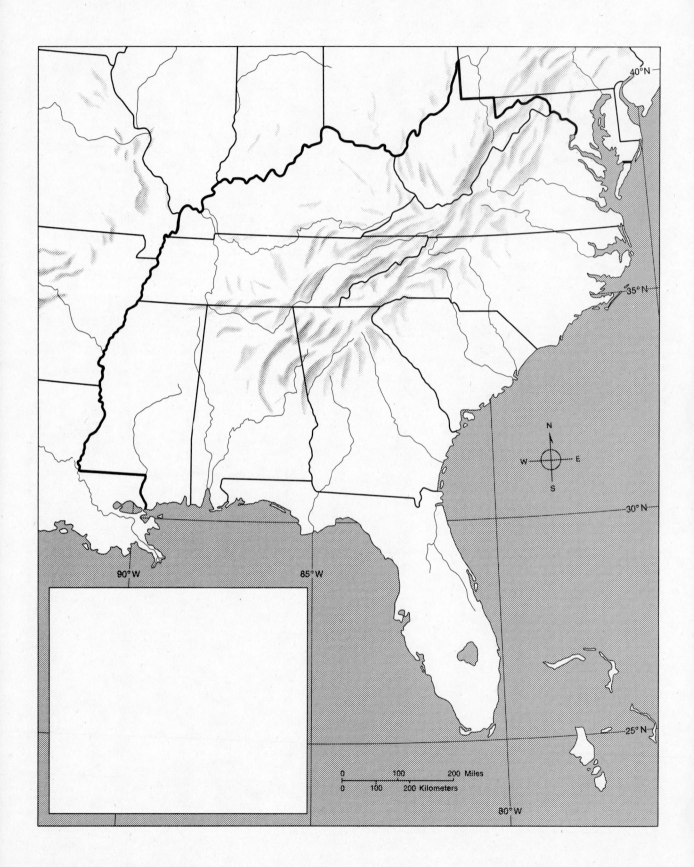

89 North Central States

90 South Central States

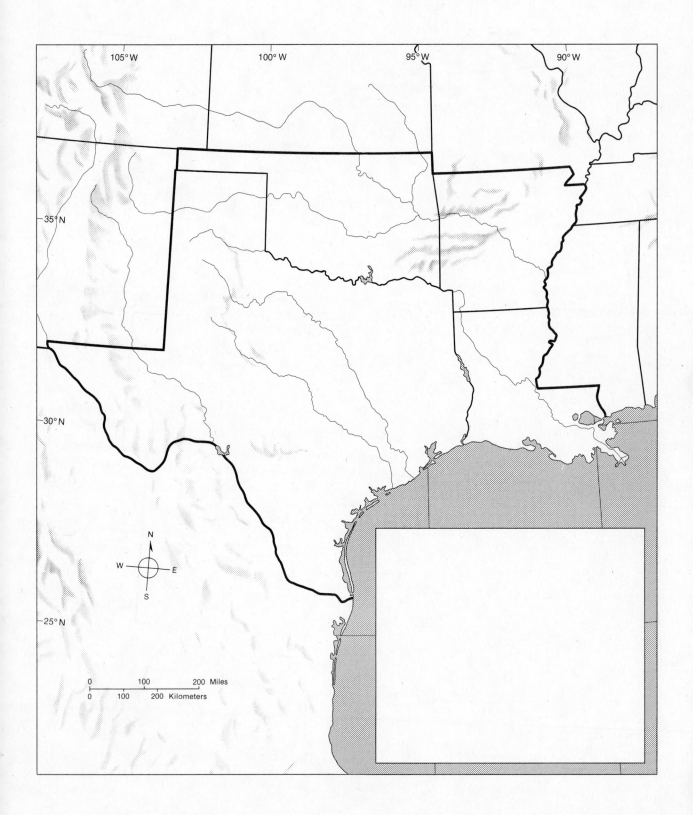

© Prentice-Hall, Inc.

91 Rocky Mountain States

92 Pacific Coast States

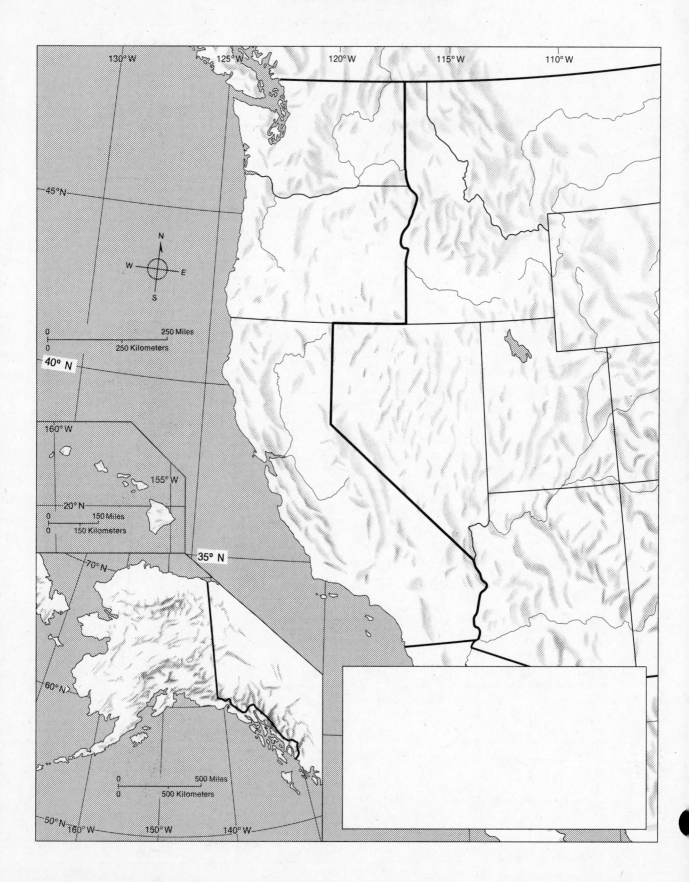